WHEN
HISTORY AND FAITH
COLLIDE

WHEN
HISTORY AND FAITH
COLLIDE

Studying Jesus

CHARLES W. HEDRICK

© 1999 by Hendrickson Publishers, Inc.
P. O. Box 3473
Peabody, Massachusetts 01961–3473
All rights reserved
Printed in the United States of America

ISBN 1–56563–235–4

First Printing — May 1999

Library of Congress Cataloging-in-Publication Data

Hedrick, Charles W.
    When history and faith collide: studying Jesus   /
Charles W. Hedrick.
    Includes bibliographical references and index.
    ISBN 1–56563–235–4
    1. Jesus Christ—Historicity.   2. Bible.   N.T.   Gospels—
Criticism, interpretation, etc.   I. Title.
    BT303.2.H43   1998
    232.9′08—dc21   98–42481
                                                    CIP

For Lorraine Shell
English Teacher Extraordinaire
An obligation long overdue

TABLE OF CONTENTS

ACKNOWLEDGMENTS

We are scarcely living in a post–Christian era, as some of the "death of God" theologians insisted in the 1960s.[1] Keen interest persists in studying Jesus, as the recent spate of books on Jesus clearly attests. On the one hand, Jesus, the Lord of Christian faith, is quite relevant in the 1990s, it turns out. On the other hand, the historicity of the character, words, and deeds of the gospels' Jesus, the man portrayed in greater than human dimensions, has been challenged by some recent publications.[2] The gap between the Jewish man and the Christian Lord, emerging in the eighteenth century, has today grown even wider. This book, growing out of classes taught during the last twenty years, aims to help beginning students appreciate the depth and width of the gap, and invites them to engage for themselves a discussion that has been taking place, out of the public eye, for some two hundred and fifty years.

Thanks to Southwest Missouri State University, which awarded me a year-long sabbatical enabling me to complete a first draft of this book. Further, I am grateful for the comments of colleagues and students who have critiqued later drafts. Six in particular should be mentioned—but not held accountable: J. Ramsey Michaels, Douglas M. Parrott, Mark Boyer, Robert Stephens, and David Trobisch. And thanks to

Jacob Harris for verifying biblical citations. Patrick Alexander, my editor at Hendrickson, has helped to shape obscure and stilted prose into a readable manuscript. To him belongs much credit; the faults are mine.

PREFACE

The Copernican theory of the nature of the universe incited a major collision between faith and history, and the scientific revolution following the collision chronicles a sad chapter in the history of human thought. What was at stake was nothing short of the nature of the physical universe itself. In the ancient world people believed the earth was the center of the universe. Claudius Ptolemaeus, an astronomer of the mid-second century C.E., formulated the classic statement of this ancient geocentric view, and it endured as the solution of science and faith until the seventeenth century C.E. Ptolemy described the earth as immobile and motionless. The sun, moon, and other planets rotated in fixed orbits around the earth. There were good, common-sense reasons for such a view. A person could stand still in the predawn hours facing east, feel the earth firm and solid underfoot, observe the gradual rising of the sun, follow its movement across the sky, and note it eventually sinking beneath the western horizon. Of course the sun moved!

Even the Christian church subscribed to this view, and it was the view of the earlier biblical writers. For example, Mark, describing the first Easter morning, said the women came to the tomb of Jesus "when the sun had risen" (Mark

2:2). According to the Hebrew Bible, Joshua commands the sun to cease its journey across the sky for a full day while the Israelites fought the Amorites (Josh 10:12–14). Theological reasons likewise seemed to point toward an earth-centered universe. God had created the earth as the first of his creative acts (Gen 1). The sun, moon, and stars are barely even mentioned (Gen 1:16). Hence the earth was the center of God's creation. God's creatures, man and woman, were given authority over the earth and all God's creation (Gen 1:26–31). Any view other than geocentrism seriously weakened humankind's pride of place in the universe, and, by implication, God's as well.

In the sixteenth century Polish scientist and churchman Nikolas Copernicus proved that the solar system was heliocentric: in short, the earth and all the planets rotated around the sun. While his views eventually became the basis for our modern view, at that time they were radically different from accepted beliefs and were regarded as heresy. Fearing the inevitable collision his views would produce, Copernicus did not publish his research until he lay dying. Copernicus was right. The earliest scholars affirming the views of Copernicus were censured by the church for their research and teaching. At the end of the sixteenth century, Giordano Bruno, an Italian monk-philosopher, was tried by church courts and given a chance to recant the views of Copernicus. When he refused, he was convicted and burned at the stake as a heretic. In the early seventeenth century Galileo Galilei, an Italian astronomer, was tried by the religious authorities and placed under house arrest. Eventually, he was forced to recant the views of Copernicus and, perjuring himself, to reaffirm the Ptolemaic view of an earth-centered universe.

Church authorities declared the view that the earth rotated around the sun as "contrary to Scripture." The very idea "that the sun was the center of the universe and is immobile is foolish and absurd in philosophy and formally heretical since it contradicts the express words of the Scriptures. . . ."[1] In spite of able arguments to the contrary, however, by the early nineteenth century all formal opposition to the view that the earth rotated around the sun ceased. Today every junior high school student knows the earth to be a planet in rotation around the sun. And as we know today, the earth is not even the center of our local solar system.

Collisions between faith and history, as this example clearly shows, do not occur without pain and significant adjustment. For many, studying Jesus as historical man rather than as divine Son of God involves an inevitable collision between history and faith, considerable emotional pain, and, if the reader perseveres, perhaps a significant adjustment of views. On a smaller scale, it is not unlike the disorientation and protests of the church of the sixteenth and seventeenth centuries caused by the collision of its faith with the views of Copernicus.

The savior worshiped in song and prayer seems so easy to understand when compared to the son of a Jewish mother whose final words from a Roman cross are in one gospel, "My God, my God, why have you forsaken me?" and in another, "Father, into your hands I commit my spirit." The effect of such discord can be devastating. Faith can be shattered, its foundations shaken, and its hopes mocked. But order can come from chaos. Studying Jesus, rather than simply affirming creedal statements learned in childhood, can bring new insights, a broader understanding, and a deeper appreciation for the complementary relationship between faith and history. For many, a more mature faith has grown out of challenging an earlier faith that has never struggled with the issues discussed in this book.

The pages that follow contend that the collision between faith and history need not be totally destructive, though some clearing of the underbrush of unexamined views must take place before new growths occur. *When History and Faith Collide* asserts that the ancient documents witnessing to Jesus of Nazareth must be studied comparatively, in contrast to each other, and analyzed as first-century writings. In short, only treating them as first-century texts will lead to a historical understanding of the public career and death of Jesus of Nazareth. The book begins with the problems, helps the reader to appreciate their significance, and then edges forward considering various solutions. The approach is inductive. The book seeks to engage students in the search for solutions, encouraging them to acknowledge the problems and resolve the difficulties for themselves.

ABBREVIATIONS

ABD   *Anchor Bible Dictionary*

BAR   *Biblical Archeology Review*

HTR   *Harvard Theological Review*

JBL   *Journal of Biblical Literature*

MDB   *Mercer Dictionary of the Bible*

NHS   Nag Hammadi Studies

NTS   *New Testament Studies*

SBLSBS   Society of Biblical Literature Sources
         for Biblical Study

SNTSMS   Society for New Testament Studies
         Monograph Series

INTRODUCTION

This book aims to be descriptive. It does not begin with answers—either religious or academic. Rather, it begins with the problems readers face when encountering the New Testament gospels in general and when studying Jesus in particular. Certain questions inevitably arise from a descriptive analysis of the early Christian gospels—if the analysis is not guided and informed by a particular religio-philosophical view of the texts. The book also aims to help students appreciate the difficulties scholars face when they try to reconstruct a historical portrait of Jesus of Nazareth from a critical analysis of the gospel texts.[1] Hence this study does not privilege the traditional orthodox view of Jesus. That view is a devout reconstruction of Jesus of Nazareth from the diverse perspectives of the canonical gospels under the influence of Christian creeds, both within the New Testament and later. Piety solves the problem of the "historical Jesus" by asserting that the orthodox Jesus of Christian faith (i.e., Jesus as he has been reconstructed by the church from canonical gospel literature under the influence of the creeds) is identical to the Jesus of history (i.e., what may be known of Jesus by the canons of scientific historical analysis).[2] It may be true, as faith asserts, that the Christ of faith and the historical Jesus are one and the same, but that assertion

may be investigated and verified or challenged by applying historical criticism to the gospels and considering other ancient evidence
for Jesus of Nazareth (the historian considers all evidence).

The purpose of reconstructing a historical portrait of Jesus of
Nazareth is not to replace the Christ of early Christian preaching
as the basis for faith. Rather, it is to determine what aspects of the
public career of Jesus have a higher degree of historical reliability,
and to evaluate the extent to which the orthodox view is grounded
in reliable historical tradition. The less the Christ of religious belief can be grounded in objective history, the more his historical
character tends to dissolve into myth. Thus the attempt to reconstruct a historical view of Jesus (i.e., one that can win the assent
of the scholar who does not reconstruct history on the basis of religious faith) becomes a principal concern for the scholar who re-
constructs history within the context of faith, as well as for the
curiosity of the secular historian.

By working through the gospels as sources for historical information rather than as repositories of divine revelation, the student
will come to appreciate the difficulties of reaching absolute conclusions about Jesus as historical man, as well as the historical difficulties inherent in the orthodox reconstruction of Jesus. Such an
approach, and its results, may well clash with the orthodox portrait of Jesus reconstructed from the canonical gospels. Therefore
some risk is involved; but there is a greater risk in not engaging the
issue of history's collision with faith. Those who never raise the
questions or face the problems base their faith on an unexamined
reconstruction developed by others. Perhaps this book can em-
power readers to begin the quest for themselves. Just gaining an
appreciation of some of the problems that have occupied scholarship for the past two hundred fifty years is an admirable beginning.

Each reader will be faced with several issues that are raised,
but not really resolved, by this study. Resolving them should actually be the reader's responsibility, since they admit of no simple
solution. (1) What constitutes the reality that human beings perceive? The gospels present modern Western readers with an ancient way of perceiving reality. Yet many modern readers insist
that the ancient view of reality presented in the gospels is actually
the way things are. Thus a key issue to be resolved is the tension
between the picture of reality in the gospels and a modern world

view. (2) History is a historian's construct. Historians do not only interpret history; they actually "create" it in their collecting and presentation of the random events of the past. This is nowhere more true than in the different portraits of Jesus of Nazareth in the four canonical gospels. What aspects of these portraits seem to have a greater grounding in historical reality? (3) A history consciously written from the perspective of the historian's faith will differ remarkably from one constructed on the basis of natural/human causation. Which of the two approaches will be most apt to reconstruct events as they would have appeared to objective observers in the past? (4) Is the value of the gospels diminished because of their diversity, their differences, and because they were themselves shaped by early Christian faith? Can one trust the gospels as historical sources for Jesus of Nazareth? To the latter question, the answer of scholarship over the last two hundred and fifty years has been both *yes* and *no.* It depends on what is being asked, and who is doing the asking.

1

HISTORY AND FAITH

Many readers of the canonical gospels (Matthew, Mark, Luke, John) tend to assume that the stories they tell took place exactly as described. When Mark's gospel, for example, says that Jesus walked on the water (Mark 6:48), some readers take it to mean exactly that: Jesus defied the laws of gravity and the properties of water, and strode across the surface of the Sea of Galilee. When Jesus is portrayed exorcising demons (Mark 5:1–20), many readers readily accept that there are, or were, "demons," and that Jesus compelled them to leave their victims. In other words, for many readers the gospels accurately describe historical reality. Yet when nonbiblical literature reports the same kind of "miraculous occurrences," readers are less willing to admit the same degree of historical probability to them.[1] For example, when the second-century Greek writer Philostratus reports that Apollonius of Tyana (a first-century figure) exorcised demons, restored sight to the blind, healed paralytics, raised a young girl from the dead, and miraculously released his own leg irons in prison, the same readers doubt the veracity of these reports.[2]

At some point miracle stories outside the Bible shade over into unreality, the bizarre, and the romantic. Readers are reluctant to take them as seriously as they do the canonical gospels. Many of the extrabiblical accounts, however, differ little from those reported about Jesus in the canonical gospels. Yet few today would seriously consider Apollonius to have performed these deeds, even though the descriptions are no more romantic than the gospel accounts. Even fourth-century Christians wrote against the exploits of Apollonius, calling him a charlatan, or a magician,[3] and they asserted that if he did achieve what is reported about him, it was only through the power of evil spirits, with whom he doubtlessly cooperated.[4]

What makes the exploits of Jesus "historical" but Apollonius's exploits not historical? Answers may vary widely. For example, people with deep faith in the Bible may respond that the reports about Jesus are true because they are in the Bible. Conversely, those about Apollonius are not. Others, with deep faith in Christianity as the "true" religion, might argue, as did Eusebius (fourth century C.E.), that such miracles could happen only at the behest of the Christian god. Still others, would insist that none of these reports are "historical," at least not by the standards of modern Western historiography. By that standard the reports in the gospels and in Philostratus (who describes the deeds of Apollonius) are the products of pious imagination, or are pious interpretations of history. In other words, history and faith collide, and appear to be two incompatible ways of reconstructing the past.

Is that true? Are history and faith essentially two different and incompatible ways of viewing reality? The answer to that question will likely depend on who responds. History purports to reconstruct events of the past.[5] Religious faith is a belief in greater-than-human powers (the gods) and their activities. Modern Western historians proceed by investigating past events, reconstructing sequences among them, and determining their relations, causes, and effects. Religious people order their behavior and have faith that events happen under the providence of their god(s) based on their confidence that greater-than-human powers (the gods) exist beyond human visual perception.

❧ MYTH, HISTORY, AND FAITH

Most people would likely agree that historical events should influence the nature of faith in some way. A faith in gods who have nothing to do with human life is mythology—stories about the gods that occur in a place and time different from common human experience. Mythical stories afford little direct information about what has taken place in the realm of human experience, but by analyzing these stories scholars may learn about the people who created and told them.[6] But divine powers and their activities such as those described in the *Theogony* by the Greek poet Hesiod, and the Babylonian creation account the *Enuma Elish*, for example, really do not impact us directly.[7] Faith in the gods may cause us to behave in particular ways (for example, in ritual and worship), but unless the gods of such stories actually act on us and our world, they do not affect us in ways beyond our control.[8] The creation accounts of Hesiod and the *Enuma Elish* are set in the primordium, i.e., their events are depicted as happening before the beginning of the world; consequently they are inappropriate sources for reconstructing either human or natural history in the sense that the word is used in modern Western historiography.

∞ THE GODS AS PLAYERS IN THE HUMAN DRAMA

Ancient writers also described human events as being influenced by the power of the gods. They portray the gods actually manipulating events to achieve a certain end. Thus the god Apollo enveloped the legendary Greek hero Aeneas in a dark cloud to protect him from death at the hands of his enemies.[9] He also knocked off the helmet of Patroclus during the battle for Troy, and as Patroclus stood there dazed by the blow from Apollo, he was wounded and killed by Hector.[10] Athena is said to have saved Achilles from death by deflecting a spear thrown by Hector.[11] In like manner, the writer of Genesis portrays the god of the Hebrews as separating the waters to deliver the Hebrews from the Egyptians (Exod 14–15).

Episodes like this recur throughout antiquity, for virtually all ancient writers thought their gods were involved in their common everyday lives.[12] Rare exceptions, however, do anticipate the way history is reconstructed in modern Western culture. As early as the fourth century B.C.E., the Greek philosopher and literary critic Aristotle advised playwrights to develop a plot for their plays (tragedies) that turned on the basis of human interaction and natural causation. Aristotle thought it undermined the believability of the dramatic presentation to invoke the gods as the cause of events in a drama.[13] Plays that appealed to divine activity to resolve the complications of plot were not as effective as those that appealed to natural causation. Aristotle did not deny the existence of the gods, but he appears to have thought people could relate more easily to a dramatic presentation that relied upon human action.

Anyone insisting that historical narratives including the activities of the gods are just as effective as those that do not, must face the questions: Whose gods are to be invoked as actors in the "historical" narrative? Whose faith perspective should guide the narrative? Of course, if the material were fiction or drama, anyone's gods can be invoked, and it would not matter. But if the writing involves recording what actually happened in the past, then the question "whose gods?" becomes significant.

ϖ THEOLOGICAL HISTORY VERSUS NONRELIGIOUS HISTORY

The question "whose gods?" is significant, for not all historians share the same religious views or worship the same gods. Since different religions have different value systems, the activity of a given religion's gods described as a part of events would be perceived differently than another's. In other words, the causes, outcomes, and significance of events in theological histories are tied to the belief systems and theology of the historians doing the writing. Under such conditions objectivity in the evaluation of events recedes and eventually is lost. For example, compare the Assyrian Sennacherib's report of his successful campaign into Palestine. He traced his victories to his god Ashur. He noted how he had taken Judah's walled cities, and, how, laying siege to Jerusalem, he shut up Judah's king Hezekiah like a "bird in a cage."[14]

The reports of the Assyrian campaign in Hebrew literature bear out Sennacherib's success (2 Kgs 18:13–19:37; Isa 36–39), but they attribute the salvation of Jerusalem to an angel of Yahweh who killed 185,000 Assyrians in one night, prompting Sennacherib to withdraw (2 Kgs 19:35; Isa 37:36). Thus the biblical narrator turns defeat into "victory."

When Sennacherib invaded Egypt, the Egyptians attributed their deliverance to the intervention of their god, who promised the Egyptian king in a dream that he would send them aid. And he did—by sending field mice who ate the Assyrians quivers, bow strings, and the leather handles of their shields. As a result the Assyrians suffered great losses and retreated.[15]

It is difficult for historians to evaluate or corroborate divine intervention in human affairs, as in the preservation of Jerusalem related above. While the author of 2 Kings clearly believed that Yahweh had delivered the city, it is by no means clear that Sennacherib would have accepted that account of the encounter. Such differences raise questions: for example, to what extent does a theological history serve the historian's religious self-interest, and to what extent does it accurately describe the causes of events? In the case of the reports of Sennacherib's campaign against Jerusalem in 2 Kings and Isaiah, it appears that the narrow escape of the city had been turned into a victory for the Judahites through the interpretation of the pious writer.

Modern Western historians, on the other hand, reconstruct and interpret history on the basis of objective criteria—criteria that can be measured by people of all faiths and nonfaiths as well. A nonreligious history consciously omits any appeal to the action of the gods and does not invoke divine intervention into human affairs to resolve them.

✽ HISTORICAL NARRATIVE AND PUBLIC EDUCATION

The differences in theological interpretation among the reports in the previous section confirm the wisdom of the First Amendment to the United States Constitution. The First Amendment mandates strict neutrality of government toward religion. Hence texts used for the study of religion in public education must reflect that same neutrality. The U.S. government cannot establish a religion or endorse one religious view over another. Hence the reconstruction of history in texts used in public education in the U.S. should not present history from the perspective of a given historian's personal religious faith. The study of the past in public education proceeds on the basis of natural causation, i.e., on the

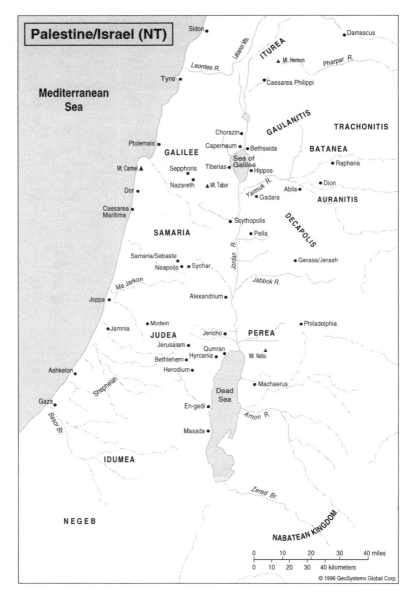

basis of forces in society such as politics, social custom, economics, natural disaster, and even religion (as analyzed descriptively and sociologically). The reason for this should be clear even to the most devout reader. If a high school history teacher happened to be Assyrian, students would undoubtedly study the siege of Jerusalem from the perspective of Sennacherib, who understood his victory to be due to his god, Ashur. If a teacher happened to be from Judah, the event would be studied from the perspective that Hezekiah's god, Yahweh, had delivered the city.

Modern historians, however, ignore the theological claims of each account as evidence for what happened, since there is no way to verify either. A modern historian is more interested in the strength of Jerusalem's walls and the security of its water supply, or in the observation that since Sennacherib received the tribute he wanted from Hezekiah (2 Kgs 18:13–16), he likely would not have wanted to waste good troops in a prolonged assault on the city. In other words, modern historians are more interested in the natural and human factors in events.[16] And if 185,000 men were actually lost in a single night, as the Hebrew account states, historians would explore natural, rather than theological, explanations for such an occurrence.[17]

∞ HISTORY AND EARLY CHRISTIANITY

Early Christians regarded the actuality of Jesus' life (i.e., the fact that he was an actual human being) as central to the Christian message. Like other people of their day, they believed their god controlled nature as well as human affairs. Hence, what happened in their lives influenced what they believed about God; and what they believed about God influenced how they perceived events. The New Testament writers insist that Jesus was a historical figure. He was not mythical, but an actual man who lived in a time and place shared with other first-century human beings. True, he was described as God's son, but he was also "born of woman, born under the law" (Gal 4:4). In the early Christian view, his human birth was the ultimate intrusion of the divine (i.e., greater-than-human powers) into a time and place that was specifically human. So closely were the circumstances of his life and human history connected that one early Christian writer, Paul, could even describe the resurrection of Jesus as the beginning of the end of human history (1 Cor 15:20–24).

The founding events of early Christianity are described as a part of the mundane affairs of Jewish history in the early Roman

Empire: Jesus was born to a Jewish woman, and grew to manhood obedient to the Jewish law (Torah); he had a public career in Galilee and Judea (political divisions of Roman Palestine); he was crucified under Pontius Pilate, a Roman prefect, and was buried; sometime later his tomb was reported empty, and early Christians proclaimed his resurrection to be God's vindication of Jesus as the anointed one of God (the Messiah; Rom 1:1–4). No matter how highly Christians of canonical New Testament literature may have exalted him, they always insisted on grounding Jesus in the mundane events of Jewish history.[18] For example, the exalted christological figure of Philippians 2:6–11 who was equal with God is much grander than the baby born in a stable (Luke 2:7), but even that exalted figure, who came from heaven and returned to heaven, humbled himself and died on a cross (cf. also Col 1:15–20). His birth, life, and death tie the Christ of religious belief to a particular period of human history. Though he may bear the very glory of God and uphold the universe by his powerful word (Heb 1:1–4), he will always be "Mary's child" (cf. John 19:25–27).

HISTORY AND FAITH IN EARLY CHRISTIANITY

As with most groups in antiquity, what early Christians believed influenced how they interpreted and reported events. Their interpretations were not merely commentary on the objective facts behind events. Rather their faith was interwoven into their narratives; the shape and scope of their reports of events were filtered through the faith of the writer. They produced not an objective history, but a history written from an overtly Christian perspective. As histories go, such a view is neither inferior nor superior; it is simply a Christian view of events. Early Christian writers made no effort to be objective or unbiased; they were writing a "theological history," an interpretation of history with a deliberate slant.

For example, most regarded the sacred books of Judaism as de facto Christian books, even though the Hebrew Bible contains the religious texts of the ancient Hebrews. Early Christians read them from the perspective of their faith that Jesus was the Messiah, i.e., the Christ. Or to put it differently: their Christ was the Messiah promised in the sacred books of Israel. The author of Matthew cites Isa 7:14, arguing that Jesus was born to a virgin because it had been "predicted" by the prophet (Matt 1:22–23)—despite the fact that Isaiah's own explanation of the sign does not agree with Matthew's interpretation of it. In Isaiah, the statement that a "young woman of marriageable age"[19] would bear a child was spoken in relation to Judah's political crisis (see Isa 7–8). According to the book of Isaiah the birth of the child was a "sign" to King Ahaz that Judah would survive the rival powers of Syria and Israel, nations that were then threatening the nation of Judah (Isa 7:14–16). The author of Matthew, though, read Isaiah's statement from the perspective of his belief that Jesus was the Messiah, and thus Isa 7:14 became a prediction of Jesus' birth. Through this kind of biblical interpretation the early Christians wrote themselves into the course of Hebrew history—or perhaps it is better to say they claimed Hebrew history as Christian history. They did not read the Hebrew Bible as a product of the past having a primary relationship to other past events of its own time. Rather, it became for them a resource for propagating Christian belief. They believed the writings of Israel were special, oracular literature[20] that anticipated the coming of Christianity. This belief controlled how the Jewish texts were read and, in turn, influenced the writing of early Christian history. For example, the author of Luke portrays Jesus near the end of his career as not being in control of his own life (Luke 22:22); rather, the events of his life were determined by God, and set forth already in the Hebrew Scripture.[21]

∞ NONRELIGIOUS HISTORIES

The earliest Christians probably would not have understood the term "history" in any modern critical sense. For them, human and natural events were not commonplace and mundane, for they believed the world and human history had been invaded by greater-than-human powers. They believed their god and other powers (for example, demons) were acting in and through human events and in natural occurrences. The same can be said about virtually every other writer in the Hellenistic period.

History in a modern sense was "invented" by the Greeks in the fifth century B.C.E., but subsequently did not continue to be written.

It was not rediscovered until the modern period. The term *history* (ἰστορία) and the idea of history reflected in the ancient historian Thucydides, and to a lesser extent in Herodotus, as a record of what actually happened do not appear in the New Testament; nor did the New Testament writers present their narratives as Thucydides did his. Thucydides describes the events of the Peloponnesian War between the Greek city-states of Athens and Sparta in the fifth century B.C.E. without mentioning any involvement of the gods. The events and causes of the war were described as strictly human and natural occurrences.[22]

The contrast between the historical reconstruction of Thucydides and what appears in the early Christian gospels can best be seen in how Thucydides treats the gods. He accurately describes the piety and impiety of the people about whom he writes, but he never describes the gods as the causes of events in the war, nor is there evidence of the miraculous like that found in the early Christian gospels.

Generally the view of ancient writers (and this includes the early Christians) was that the natural world and human events are not what they appear to be on the surface; rather, they are the arenas in which the powers of evil and righteousness clash, where the gods are involved in human events in a direct way—such as one finds in the Bible. This ancient view is still held by many today: God moves in history and is working to bring all things to a satisfactory conclusion.

When the Roman Empire fell in 410 C.E., Augustine wrote *The City of God* as an apologetic for God's ultimate victory in the world. This book has been described as "the beginning of the teleological interpretation of history."[23] The view that history served the providence of god (or some other eternal principle) formed the pattern for historiography during the Middle Ages and beyond. Purely secular views of history were not written until the late eighteenth and the nineteenth centuries.[24] A strictly secular view of history focuses on a natural cause/effect scheme for the way events proceed; it does not seek an eternal meaning to history. Such an approach has the advantage of focusing on the causes of events that are evident to both the believer and the nonbeliever alike.

⚘ THEOLOGICAL HISTORIES

Histories written from a theological perspective are guided by the belief of the historian, particularly when the history touches on basic matters of faith held by the historian's community. For example, the confession that "Jesus is the Christ, the Son of God" is shared by most mainstream Christian groups. Most assume that Jesus presented himself as the Christ during his earthly life. Yet in the canonical gospels Jesus is never portrayed as unambiguously claiming this for himself. Nonetheless, it is a claim clearly made for him by characters in the canonical gospels, by the gospel writers themselves, and by other early Christian authors.[25] On the one hand, someone guided by the belief of the church would be inclined to read the gospel accounts in line with standard confessions and thus would find little discrepancy between the authors' and characters' claims about Jesus, and the claims that Jesus is represented as making about himself. Having a high view of the historical value of the gospels and a belief in their authors as "inspired" removes any disparity between Jesus' own claims and those made about him by others.

On the other hand, a historian whose reconstruction of early Christian history is uninfluenced by the confession of the church might see here a significant difference and conclude that Jesus did not specifically claim to be the Christ or Son of God during his lifetime. Such a historian might regard the claim that Jesus was the Son of God as an evaluation of Jesus influenced by the belief that God raised him from the dead. Furthermore, such a historian might therefore consider the possibility that the earthly life of Jesus was not "christological." But the historian whose reconstruction of history is shaped by the classical Christian creeds[26] will have ruled out such a possibility. In any case, a historian who tries to be objective would preserve the distinctions in the way the christological titles are applied to Jesus in the gospels. A historian who writes history from the perspective of the creeds and a personal belief in Jesus as the Son of God would tend to ignore the differences.

In the canonical gospels a human being of the first quarter of the first century is described from multiple faith perspectives by

Christians of the latter half of the first century. Their writings are a blend of faith and history. The portrayal of events of Jesus' life and death are colored by later beliefs about him. They made no attempt to keep their faith out of the gospels. Hence their record of Jesus of Nazareth is not a historical account in the narrow sense of a modern historiography that describes causality and the linking of events on the basis of natural causes.

⚬⚬ THE HISTORIAN, THE NOVELIST, AND THE EVANGELIST

What has been said thus far might lead a reader to think of the gospels as inferior to nonreligious histories. That is not the point. Actually the historian, the novelist, and the evangelist all prepare their narratives in the same way. They all bring order out of the chaos of random events by imposing a plan on them.[27] The historian works with real events of the past and connects them on the basis of natural or human causality. The novelist works with imaginary or real events and connects them according to the novelist's own invented plot. The evangelist works with events of the past that have been shaped by the faith of the community and connects them according to that particular evangelist's own theological purpose. The historian writes to show what happened and how it happened; the novelist writes, in general, to entertain; and the evangelist writes to persuade. All three create the sequence of their narratives according to their agendas. Each writer must be appreciated in line with his or her unique reason for writing and in terms of how effectively each attains that goal.

As literature, the gospels stand somewhere between a mythical view of "history" and modern historiography. They are neither history in a modern sense nor completely mythological—or, rather, they are both history and mythology.[28] Northrop Frye might well have called John's gospel mythical, since in John, Jesus is presented as "superior in *kind* both to other men and to the environment" (Frye's standard for describing myth). The prologue of John portrays Jesus as a preexistent eternal figure whose "signs" demonstrate his power over the environment. According to Frye, the heroes of narratives of this sort are divine beings, and the stories about them will be a myth in the common sense of a story about a god.[29]

Jesus, however, is also clearly presented in the canonical gospels as a human being. He is born to a human mother (Matthew and Luke), suffers (all four gospels), and is firmly bound to the world in a way that the classic gods of the Greeks and Romans are not. In the gospels Jesus is more like the Greek hero Herakles (the Roman, Hercules) than Zeus, for example. Zeus is one of the Greek eternal deities, while Herakles, his son, is (like Jesus) described as a human being with an earthly mother and a heavenly father. Hence, in Frye's categories the gospels could well be "romance," if one decided that Jesus is portrayed there as "superior in *degree* to other men and the environment" (Frye's standard for describing romance). The hero of the romance is portrayed as a human being "whose actions are marvelous." He "moves in a world where the ordinary laws of nature are slightly suspended: prodigies of courage and endurance, unnatural to us are natural to him, and enchanted weapons, talking animals, terrifying ogres and witches and talismans of miraculous power"[30] all form part of the supernatural world of the romance. Basically the gospels describe a human being as a divine figure. Such a blend of the human and the divine generally characterized history writing until the emergence of a scientific sense of history during the Renaissance.[31]

2

JESUS AND THE GOSPELS IN THE TWENTIETH CENTURY

To judge from their writings, early Christians began describing historical facets of the life of Jesus about a quarter century after his death. As far as we know, Paul, the earliest known Christian author and a contemporary of Jesus, described only six aspects of Jesus' life: he was descended from David (Rom 1:3); was born to a woman under the authority of the Jewish Torah (Gal 4:4); had a brother, James (Gal 1:19); ate a special meal with his followers the night before he died (1 Cor 11:23–25); was crucified (Gal 3:1) and buried (1 Cor 15:4). But these six incidental bits of information scarcely constitute a "life." What was really important for Paul was that Jesus was the resurrected Lord who dwelled in the believer's heart (Gal 2:20). A reading of the undisputed letters of Paul[1] shows that Paul either knows little about the circumstances of the life of the historical man or does not regard such information important, or both.[2] The early Christian gospel texts, both canonical and noncanonical, are virtually the only sources for detailed information about the historical man. But even these earliest attempts to anchor the church's gospel in the life of the historical man tend to obscure Jesus as a historical figure.

Two hundred fifty years of analytical historical study and almost two thousand years of confessional reflection have failed to produce a single description of Jesus that commands the general support of either critical New Testament scholarship or the church. The failure to agree on a historical description of Jesus raises, in turn, questions about the church's theological reconstructions of Jesus' person and career. One reason for the failure to produce a uniform, or near uniform, description is that the "earliest lives" (Matthew, Mark, Luke, and John) present diverging portraits of Jesus. Each attempts to provide a historical context for how the church's gospel began, and each affirms in different ways that the resurrected Christ and Lord of Christian faith was at the same time Jesus of Nazareth, a Jew who had lived in a Roman province on the periphery of the Roman Empire. In a sense, the gospels are the earliest attempts to recover the life of the historical man, although what they produce are narratives that blend both historical information (i.e., that which could have been verified by a disinterested party, if present) and confessional perception. They, as well as other early gospel literature, view the life of the historical man through the filter of Christian faith in him as the resurrected Son of God. These narratives do not agree in all their historical particulars or theological perceptions.

✂ THE OLD QUEST FOR THE HISTORICAL JESUS

Systematic analytical study of Jesus of Nazareth did not begin until the middle of the eighteenth century with the work of the German scholar, Hermann Samuel Reimarus (1694–1768).[3] The Old Quest was distinctly a German quest. British and French scholars continued to produce traditional Protestant "lives of Jesus" under the assumption that the gospels were objective biography. Reimarus's study of Jesus broke with this view and was so innovative and challenging to the traditional pietistic view of Jesus that Reimarus did not allow it to be published during his lifetime (all of it has never been published). After his death seven excerpts from his manuscript were published (1774–1778) as the "Wolfenbüttel

Fragments." In the seventh "fragment" ("The Aims of Jesus and His Disciples") Reimarus essentially argued that there is a difference between what Jesus himself taught and what his followers taught about him. In other words, an embarrassing gap existed between what Jesus preached (i.e., God's kingdom) and what his followers preached (i.e., Jesus as the Son of God). This gap remains the essential problem of historical Jesus research today: to what extent do the early Christian interpretations of Jesus (i.e., the gospels) have a firm basis in the life of the historical man? To put the question somewhat differently: are there correlations between the Christ of Christian faith, as he is presented in the gospels, and Jesus of Nazareth, as he can be reconstructed using critical historical methods?

In 1835 another German scholar, David Friedrich Strauss, published a study on Jesus entitled, *The Life of Jesus Critically Examined.* Strauss compared the gospels to other religious literature in antiquity, examining what he called "sacred history," or "a history of events in which the divine enters . . . into the human [realm]" (p. 39). These sacred histories with their legends and stories in which human history was invaded by divine figures Strauss termed "myths." Although the gospels contained history, Strauss asserted, they most assuredly presented Jesus in "mythical garb," exactly as had been done in the legends and stories of the sacred histories of antiquity. For Strauss, myth was not a historical description but a pious fiction. The gospels were early Christian ways of thinking about Jesus that presented him in greater-than-human dimensions. Once the mythical garb is removed, however, these legends and myths, with which the canonical gospels clothed the historical man, may have a historical memory at their base. But for Strauss, in their present condition the gospels were not historical presentations of Jesus; they were, rather, mythical interpretations, like the sacred histories of antiquity. Indeed in the early period of the Christian movement, according to Strauss, historical presentations would have been impossible.

In the years following Reimarus and Strauss, numerous studies on Jesus were published from both critical[4] and confessional stances. These types of studies endeavored to set out a reliable description of Jesus as a figure of human history; nevertheless, they differ to an incredible degree. At the turn of the twentieth century two books appeared that would significantly alter "history of Jesus" research. The later of these, written in 1906, was by Albert Schweitzer: *The Quest of the Historical Jesus* (*Von Reimarus zu Wrede*, "From Reimarus to Wrede"). Schweitzer surveyed the scholarly books written in the period from Hermann Samuel Reimarus (1774–1778) to Wilhelm Wrede (1901). His survey demonstrates that virtually any kind of a "life of Jesus" can be written—given the character of the early Christian gospels. That observation remains the enduring legacy of his book.

The earlier of these two books was published in 1901 by Wilhelm Wrede: *The Messianic Secret* (*Das Messiasgeheimnis in den Evangelien*, "The Messianic Secret in the Gospels"). Wrede's book was the last study that Schweitzer considered in his own book. Wrede argued that the attempts of Jesus to silence disciples and demons, who knew his true identity as Son of God, was actually Mark's literary creation to accommodate the fact (according to Wrede) that Jesus was not recognized as divine until *after* the church had come to believe in his resurrection. Hence, the "messianic secret" was not a secret initiated by Jesus, but rather it was a literary fiction invented by Mark. Schweitzer, however, disagreed with Wrede and affirmed the gospels as "historical" reports that could be used to write a historical description of Jesus. Schweitzer's own description of Jesus comes at the end of his book in a chapter entitled "Thoroughgoing Scepticism and Thoroughgoing Eschatology." Schweitzer asserts Jesus to be an eschatological[5] prophet who expected the end of the world in his own lifetime. In other words, Jesus' message that the kingdom of God was imminent was to be understood as a part of late Jewish apocalyptic expectation.[6]

These two books have continued to influence critical New Testament scholarship to the present day. Over the next fifty years following Schweitzer and Wrede, only two critical lives of Jesus were written, both products of German New Testament scholarship. The first was Rudolf Bultmann's *Jesus and the Word* (New York: Scribners, 1934 [German, 1926]). Bultmann does not provide a sequential course to the life of Jesus, but focuses on his words. The second was Günther Bornkamm's *Jesus of Nazareth* (London: Hodder & Stoughton, 1960 [German, 1956]). Bornkamm summarizes in one brief chapter (ch. 3) the residue of "biographical" data that can be distilled from all sources, and, like Bultmann, Bornkamm also focused on the words of Jesus. What was left of Jesus after these fifty-odd years were only his sayings—as sifted and evaluated by the historian. A traditional biography of Jesus was not thought to be possible given the nature of the gospel literature—the legacy of Schweitzer endured.

In general, critical scholars affirmed Schweitzer's emphasis on the apocalyptic element in the gospels as the historical context for the life of the historical man, and until recently they have chosen the apocalyptic sayings of Jesus as the place to begin his historical description. Other scholars, however, remain skeptical of the historical reliability of the gospel presentations of Jesus of Nazareth. It is not that the gospels do not *contain* historical material; rather, their portraits of Jesus are not reliable as biographical descriptions of the historical man. Today critical scholarship continues to focus on the words of Jesus, largely ignoring their literary settings and interpretations in the gospels, which are thought to be invented by the evangelists.

One of the results of the Old Quest was the marginalizing and eventually the disenfranchising of the Gospel of John as a reliable source for the historical Jesus. This was due, at least in part, to Schweitzer's contention that Jesus should be understood in terms of Jewish apocalypticism. The focus on apocalyptic by critical scholarship led to John's demise as a source for the historical Jesus, for John does not portray Jesus as an apocalyptic prophet. Also the Jesus of John's gospel does not have at the center of his message the nearness of the kingdom of God, as does the Jesus of the other three gospels. A majority of New Testament scholars regard the "kingdom of God" as the essential feature of Jesus' preaching. Recent research, however, focusing on wisdom traditions in early Christian and Jewish literature, has argued that Jesus can also be understood in terms of these wisdom traditions as the emissary of "Lady Wisdom."[7] For many scholars the focus on wisdom traditions has tended to weaken the view that Jesus was an apocalyptic prophet. One result of this shift in focus is a renewed interest in examining the Gospel of John for traditional wisdom motifs that John may have used in developing the Johannine portrait of Jesus.

∞ THE NEW QUEST FOR THE HISTORICAL JESUS

Schweitzer's book effectively ended the Old Quest for the historical Jesus, which, broadly speaking, sought to write a life of Jesus under the assumption that the gospels are objective biography. A New Quest opened in the middle of the twentieth century, about fifty years after Schweitzer's book had demonstrated the impossibility of the task under then current methodology. Ironically the new quest for the historical Jesus was initiated by the students of Rudolf Bultmann (1884–1976), professor of New Testament at the German University of Marburg. Bultmann had earlier denied both the possibility and the necessity for the quest. Around 1950 these first-generation students of Bultmann had risen to prominent positions in German theological education. With students of their own, they now took up a new quest for the historical Jesus.

Nevertheless the New Quest, like the Old Quest, focused on the words, or "sayings," of Jesus. Scholars were not writing biographies of Jesus in a traditional sense because the gospels were viewed more as evangelistic tracts than as historical biography. In their view the goal of the gospel authors was not to present an objective, unbiased biography of Jesus of Nazareth; rather, they wrote to solicit faith in Jesus as the Son of God. Hence the historian had to allow for this confessional prejudice of the gospel writers. Scholars still thought, however, that if Jesus' sayings could be reconstructed from their various versions in the gospels, then it was possible to describe his intentions, his aims, the focus of his being. In other words, the interpreter could determine how Jesus understood himself. A careful examination of Jesus' words, these scholars felt, afforded a new access to understanding Jesus as a historical man; it was an "existential" access that did not depend on the preaching of the early Christian church, which had portrayed Jesus as divine.

∞ OTHER DEVELOPMENTS IN GOSPEL RESEARCH IN THE TWENTIETH CENTURY

Several other developments in the first half of the twentieth century and later reinforced this approach to the gospel literature. The gospels came to be viewed as deposits of traditional material that had circulated in the early Christian communities in an oral form until they were collected and written down a generation or so later. The evangelists collected and adapted these stories and sayings in order to address the religious needs of the faith communities for which they wrote. But the sayings and stories had also been similarly adapted before the evangelists collected and recorded them. Hence the written versions of the gospels reflect adaptation to several different cultural and theological stages in the church's life.

German scholarship termed such an approach to the gospel literature *Formgeschichte*, "[a study of] the history of forms," or, as it unfortunately came to be known in the English-speaking world, "form criticism." Form-critical study compares specific literary forms in the gospel literature, such as a miracle story (e.g., Mark 9:14–29=Matt 17:14–21=Luke 9:37–43), to similar stories throughout Hellenistic antiquity.[8] Form critics attempt to reconstruct the evolution of these literary forms from earlier, simpler forms to later, more complex forms. They also project hypothetical social contexts in which the early Christian communities, as well as other groups, might have used such literary forms. For example, one might reasonably expect to find prayers (such as the Lord's Prayer) to be a product of early Christian worship. This approach enables the scholar to identify earlier forms of the tradition preceding the writing of the gospels. But it weakens the value of the gospel interpretations of Jesus as reliable sources for writing a life of Jesus. From such a perspective, the gospel writers become simply collectors and interpreters of earlier traditions about Jesus rather than actors in the founding events they report. One finding of this approach is that the Jesus traditions prior to the writing of the gospels preserved no sequential plan of his life. The structures of the gospel narratives derive from the gospel writers, who presumably developed their plans from early Christian preaching (cf., e.g., the structure of the sermons in Acts 1–12).[9]

In addition to studying the traditional literary forms in the synoptic gospels (viz., parables, proverbs, aphorisms, miracle stories, pronouncement stories, etc.) scholars also began to study their literary settings, noting how each evangelist revised the traditional material. For example, the Lost Sheep parable appears in

Matthew (18:12–13) and Luke (15:4–6). But their respective narra-tive settings differ. In Matthew the parable appears in a "speech" Jesus makes to the disciples (18:1–19:1); in Luke, Jesus responds with the parable when scribes and Pharisees accuse him of violat-ing Pharisaic dietary rules (15:1–3). Each evangelist also draws dif-ferent conclusions from the story. Matthew, in keeping with the setting of the speech made to the disciples, takes the parable to be an assurance to disciples that God will preserve even the most in-significant disciple in the community of faith (18:14). Luke, by contrast, in keeping with Jesus' defense of his dining with tax collec-tors and sinners, takes the parable to be an example of God's con-cern for the "lost" (15:7). Further, each evangelist has revised the story according to a particular understanding of it. For example, Luke describes a celebration where the shepherd "rejoices with friends and neighbors" (15:6); this feature is lacking in Matthew.

This kind of approach to the gospel literature was called *Redaktionsgeschichte*, "redaction criticism," "[a study of] the his-tory of the editing [of a given traditional unit]." This approach led to a reduced confidence in the gospels as historical sources, since the gospels were seen as theological interpretations of Jesus writ-ten under the influence of early Christian faith.

One development in the history of Jesus research has been the discovery of new gospel literature and fragments of other early Christian gospels. Some of the most significant discoveries oc-curred as recently as the middle of this century. The best known of these early Christian noncanonical gospel texts is the *Gospel of Thomas*. This text, preserved in several Greek fragments and in a complete Coptic recension, is a collection of Jesus' sayings (and a few narratives). It is not a "narrative gospel" that presents a *story* about Jesus; rather, it is a "sayings gospel" in which the sayings have minimal narrative context. For the most part, the sayings in the *Gospel of Thomas* are connected to one another by the simple repetitive statement, "Jesus said."

The significance of the *Gospel of Thomas* for the history of Jesus research is debated, but a growing number of scholars find it highly significant. It attests to the existence of early Christians who conceived of Jesus as a teacher of wisdom rather than as a crucified Lord. Also absent from this gospel are the usual confessional narratives about Jesus: virgin birth (Matthew and Luke), preexistence (John), miracles tradition (all four), crucifixion (all four), and resurrection (all four). In the *Gospel of Thomas* Jesus is known through his words rather than by his deeds. Since the *Gospel of Thomas* shares many sayings with the canonical gospels, scholars have vigorously discussed its relationship to the canonical gospels. While the issue has not been resolved to the satisfaction of many scholars, to others the *Gospel of Thomas* appears to represent the sort of undifferentiated oral tradition from which the canonical gospels would have drawn their materials. Thus it does not, as a document, appear to depend on the canonical gospels. If that is the case, for the first time since the first century there is available an access to a stage of the Jesus tradition that was suppressed by early Christians who understood Jesus in terms of crucifixion and resurrection. In any case, because of the close parallels to the sayings traditions in Matthew, Mark, and Luke, no serious study of Jesus can afford to ignore the *Gospel of Thomas* or the other early gospel texts discovered in this century.[10]

Another key issue facing any critical approach to the gospels concerns the striking similarity (sometimes virtual verbatim agreement) and equally striking diversity among the first three gospels, Matthew, Mark, and Luke. On the one hand, their views of the Jesus tradition are so similar that they are called the "synoptic gospels" (i.e., their "optic" [view] is "synonymous"), meaning that they present the career of Jesus in a similar way. On the other hand, their diversity can sometimes shock people who have never before studied these texts comparatively. Scholars refer to the complex diversity and similarity among Matthew, Mark, and Luke as the *synoptic problem*. Simply stated, the problem is: how can the relationships among these texts be explained? How one answers this significant question determines how one writes the history of early Christianity. To a great extent it will determine how the historical Jesus will be understood.

Recently, gospel research has begun to examine the gospels as literary narrative and the gospel writers as authors, rather than simply as compilers and disinterested interpreters of traditional material. Rather, researchers focus on the "story" of a particular evangelist. This approach tends to apply the conventions of modern literary criticism to the narrative, i.e., to analyze it as a self-contained literary unit with a unique narrative strategy. Such an analysis focuses on such aspects as voices in the narrative, plot, character development, narrative time, and implied readers. Reading the narrative in this way suspends the question of historicity and bypasses many other historical issues.

∞ AUTHORSHIP AND DATE OF THE GOSPELS

Students never before exposed to a critical study of the New Testament can be frequently dismayed by its methods. The methodology calls into question the traditional view that the canonical gospels were written by eyewitnesses and that the gospel writers are the persons named in their titles. Hence such critical analytical study of the gospels can be disturbing.

Modern critical scholarship generally dates all four canonical gospels between 70 and 90 C.E., forty to sixty years after Jesus' death. Mark is generally regarded as the earliest, and John the latest. There is disagreement, of course, as to their sequence, but the earliest date given for any of them is generally 65–70 C.E.[11]

All documents are dated on the basis of internal and external evidence. *Internal evidence* is any feature within a document that can be connected with an absolute system of dating outside the document. This datable reference establishes the earliest possible date of composition for the document (i.e., its *terminus a quo*), since the document could not have been written *earlier* than that datable reference. For example, a document that mentions the Japanese attack on Pearl Harbor could not have been written earlier than December 7, 1941; it could only have been written later.

The only event in the gospels that is datable on the basis of outside evidence is the destruction of the Jewish temple in the fall of 70 C.E. by the Roman general Titus and the Tenth Roman Legion (Mark 13:1–2=Matt 24:1–2=Luke 21:5–6; cf. John 2:18–20 and also Luke 21:20). Some take this allusion to the destruction of the temple as a deliberate prediction on the part of Jesus or the gospel writers.[12] That being the case, the earliest gospel could have been composed sometime prior to 70 C.E. But how much earlier? Some scholars take 70 C.E. as the earliest possible date for the composition of the first gospel. Others, allowing for Mark's "insightful intuition" into the political situation of Palestine in the second half of the first century date it around 65–70, or earlier.

External evidence for dating does not move composition of the gospels any earlier. External evidence for the date of the gospels is of two types: dated manuscripts of the gospels, and allusions in other writings. Both types come from a period later than the first century. Except for a few fragments of gospels from the second century, virtually all of the manuscripts of the gospels date from the third century and later. A fragment of the Gospel of John ($\mathfrak{P}$52=John Rylands papyrus manuscript 52 containing John 18:31–33, 37–38) is the earliest and has been dated to the first quarter of the second century. The latest date for the composition of the Gospel of John on the basis of external evidence is established with this fragment.

A second kind of external evidence involves the mention of a writing in the work of another datable writing. Unquestionably by the end of the second century the canonical gospels were known and used by the church. Irenaeus, for example, in *Against Heresies* (ca. 180) quotes from all the canonical gospels. These quotations read the same as the gospels now in use by the church, showing that he knew them. Hence, ca. 180 C.E. is a sure *terminus ad quem* for the gospels; it is the latest date the gospels could have been composed. The situation earlier in the second century is not as clear. Gospel texts cited in this period do not exactly follow the gospels currently in use today. In other cases, gospel material that can be identified with a gospel currently in use is not identified as coming from a specifically named gospel text. And finally, in some cases gospel material is cited as coming from "the Lord" rather than from a written document, suggesting it may have been cited from memory. For example, *2 Clement* (ca. 150 C.E.) quotes the Lord as saying: "Not everyone who says to me Lord, Lord shall be saved, but the one doing righteousness" (*2 Clem.* 4.2). Among the canonical gospels this saying is most like Matt 7:21: "Not everyone who says to me Lord, Lord shall enter the kingdom of heaven, but the one doing the will of my Father who is in heaven." And another: "For the Lord says in the Gospel, 'If you did not guard that which is small, who shall give you that which is great? For I tell you that he who is faithful in that which is least, is faithful also in that which is much" (*2 Clem.* 8.5). Among the gospels this is most like Luke 16:10–12: "He who is faithful in a very little is faithful also in much; and he who is dishonest in a very little is dishonest also in much. If then you have not been faithful in the unrighteous mammon, who will entrust to you the true riches? And if you have not been faithful in that which is another's, who will give you that which is your own?" (cf. Matt 25:21; Luke 19:17).[13] Thus the results are somewhat unclear. While the canonical gospels may have been known and used in the period 100–180, their titles (or authors) in this period are either unknown, or considered unimportant by the church. Quite likely they circulated anonymously; that would account for the fact that they are not ascribed to a specific author during this period. In any case the latest possible date for their composition on the basis of external evidence is ca. 100–180.

The idea that the canonical evangelists were eyewitnesses is not shared by the earliest Christians who mention these texts at the end of the second century. The suprascript titles of the gospels that attribute authorship to Matthew, Mark, Luke, and John constitute a later way of entitling documents. The earliest titles were usually derived from the first line of a given text, its incipit. Compare, for example, the title of the first book in the Christian Old Testament. What the English translates as "Genesis," derives from the Septuagint, the (Jewish) Greek translation of the Hebrew Bible. In the Hebrew Bible the earliest title of the first book is the Hebrew word *berešît*. It is the first word in the Hebrew Bible and means "in beginning." The title in the Septuagint constitutes a later reflection on the contents of the book, and means "origin."[14]

If that was also the case with these earliest gospels, their earliest titles may well have been as follows. Mark: "Beginning of the Gospel" (1:1); Matthew: "Book of the Beginning of Jesus Christ" (1:1); Luke: "In the Days of Herod" (1:5, thus eliminating the prologue 1:1–4); and John: "The Testimony of John" (1:19, thus eliminating the prologue 1:1–18).

The earliest tradition about Mark comes from Eusebius, a church writer of the early fourth century. Eusebius quoted the writings of Papias, who lived in the first half of the second century. Papias describes Mark as receiving his information from

Peter, rather than from Jesus, for Mark "was not a hearer or fol-
lower of the Lord" (Eusebius, *Ecclesiastical History* 3.39.15). In the
prologue (1:1–4) to the gospel that bears the name "Luke" the author is specifically distinguished from those who witnessed the
events described in the gospel. The reader is told that the author
had access to "many" narratives as well as the oral reports of
"those who from the beginning were eyewitnesses" (1:1–2). The
narrator of the Gospel of John is distinguished from the "beloved
disciple," who is cited as the eyewitness of the events of that gospel. John 19:35 and 21:24 describe the eyewitness as a third party
distinct from the voice that narrates the events of the gospel.[15] The
earliest tradition about Matthew describes it as a collection of Hebrew "oracles," i.e., a collection of sayings or discourses (Papias;
in Eusebius, *Ecclesiastical History* 3.39.15). This description distin-
guishes Papias's document from our Greek narrative gospel bearing the name of Matthew. Our present version of Matthew is a
narrative as opposed to a collection of sayings.

I also consider the *Gospel of Thomas* to be one of the early Christian "gospels." Its dating has not been resolved to every scholar's satisfaction, but its original composition has been dated anywhere from
50 to 140, or roughly contemporary with the composition and final
standardization of the canonical gospels themselves. The earliest reference to the *Gospel of Thomas* in patristic literature comes at the beginning of the third century C.E. (ca. 200),[16] thus providing the latest
possible date for its composition (i.e., the *terminus ad quem*). *Thomas*'s
external attestation as an early gospel is thus roughly comparable to
the canonical gospels. Also, as in the canonical gospels, the narrator
does not claim to have been an eyewitness to events in the life of the
historical Jesus.[17]

∞

This chapter has traced the developments in New Testament
studies affecting the way gospel literature is evaluated as sources
for Jesus of Nazareth. This survey is intended to alert readers to issues raised by others who have studied gospel literature in this
century. The recommended reading list provides additional details
on these and other issues to facilitate class discussion.

∞ RECOMMENDED READING AND SOURCES CONSULTED

I. General
FULLER, REGINALD H. "New Testament Theology." Pages 565–84 in *The New Testament and Its Modern Interpreters*. Edited by Eldon Epp and George W. MacRae. Atlanta: Scholars Press, 1989. RICHES, JOHN. "Quest for the Historical Jesus." *ABD* 3:796–802.

II. The Old Quest for the Historical Jesus
SCHWEITZER, ALBERT. *The Quest of the Historical Jesus*. Translated by W. Montgomery. London: A. & C. Black, 1910. TALBERT, CHARLES H. *Reimarus: Fragments*. Translated by R. S. Fraser. Philadelphia: Fortress, 1970. WREDE, WILHELM. *The Messianic Secret*. Translated by J. C. G. Greig. 1901 Reprint. Greenwood, S.C.: Attic Press, 1971.

III. The New Quest for the Historical Jesus
FUNK, R. W., and ROY W. HOOVER. *The Five Gospels: The Search for the Authentic Words of Jesus*. New York: Macmillan, 1993. KÄSEMANN, ERNST. "Blind Alleys in the 'Jesus of History' Controversy." Pages 23–65 in *New Testament Questions of Today*. Translated by W. J. Montague. Philadelphia: Fortress, 1969. KÄSEMANN, ERNST. "The Problem of the Historical Jesus." Pages 15–47 in *Essays on New Testament Themes*. Translated by W. J. Montague. SBT 41. London: SCM Press, 1964. ROBINSON, JAMES M. *The New Quest of the Historical Jesus*. SBT 25. London: SCM Press, 1959.

IV. Form and Redaction Criticism
BAILEY, JAMES L., and LYLE D. VANDER BROEK. *Literary Forms in the New Testament: A Handbook*. Louisville: Westminster John Knox, 1992. McKNIGHT, EDGAR V. "Form and Redaction Criticism." Pages 149–74 in Epp and MacRae, eds., *The New Testament and Its Modern Interpreters*. McKNIGHT, EDGAR V. *What Is Form Criticism?* Philadelphia: Fortress, 1969. PERRIN, NORMAN. *What Is Redaction Criticism?* Philadelphia: Fortress, 1969.

V. John and the Synoptic Gospels
BRIGGS, R. C. *Interpreting the New Testament Today*. Nashville: Abingdon, 1973. Pages 179–83, 228–49. HEDRICK, C. W. "The Tyranny of the Synoptic Jesus." *Semeia* 44 (1988): 1–8. KÜMMEL, W. G. *Introduction to the New Testament*. Translated by H. C. Kee. Rev. ed. Nashville: Abingdon, 1973.

VI. Noncanonical Gospel Literature
CAMERON, RON. *The Other Gospels*. Philadelphia: Westminster, 1982. MILLER, R. J., ed. *The Complete Gospels*. Sonoma, Calif.: Polebridge, 1992. SCHNEEMELCHER, WILLIAM and R. McL. WILSON, eds. *New Testament Apocrypha. Vol. 1: Gospels and Related Writings*. 2d ed. Louisville: Westminster John Knox, 1991. STROKER, W. D. *Extracanonical Sayings of Jesus*. SBLSBS 18. Atlanta: Scholars Press, 1984.

VII. The Synoptic Problem

(The literature on this topic is extensive. The bibliography that follows simply addresses the basic issues.) KÜMMEL, *Introduction to the New Testament*, 38–80. SANDERS. E. P., and MARGARET DAVIES. *Studying the Synoptic Gospels*. London: SCM Press, 1989. TYSON, J. B. *The New Testament and Early Christianity*. New York: Macmillan, 1984.

VIII. Authorship and Date of the Gospels

KÜMMEL. *Introduction to the New Testament*, 80–151, 188–247. TYSON. *The New Testament and Early Christianity*, 158–98.

IX. Myth and the New Testament

BULTMANN. RUDOLF. *Jesus Christ and Mythology*. London: SCM Press, 1964. STRAUSS. D. F. *The Life of Jesus Critically Examined*. Edited by P. C. Hodgson. Translated by George Eliot. Philadelphia: Fortress, 1972 [German 1835].

X. Literary Criticism and the New Testament

BEARDSLEE. WILLIAM. "Recent Literary Criticism." Pages 175–98 in Epp and MacRae, *The New Testament and Its Modern Interpreters*. CULPEPPER, R. A. *Anatomy of the Fourth Gospel: A Study in Literary Design*. Philadelphia: Fortress, 1983. RHOADS, DAVID, and DONALD MICHIE. *Mark as Story: An Introduction to the Narrative of a Gospel*. Philadelphia: Fortress, 1982. TALBERT, CHARLES H. *Reading Luke: A Literary and Theological Commentary*. New York: Crossroad, 1982.

∞ ISSUES FOR STUDY AND DISCUSSION

1. Summarize Reimarus's evidence for assuming that there is a discrepancy between what Jesus preached and what the church preached about him. Does there appear to be a difference? What conclusions if any can be drawn from that?

2. What did Strauss mean by myth? Give two examples of myth from ancient texts other than the New Testament; give two examples from the gospels with specific reference to Jesus. Would Strauss classify your examples as myth? Do you agree or disagree with Strauss? Why? Assume that it is myth; how would that assumption color one's understanding of the gospel literature?

3. Describe Schweitzer's view of Jesus. What is Schweitzer's evidence for his conclusion that Jesus thought the world would actually end in his lifetime? Is there evidence in the gospels that this is not the case?

4. Why do critical scholars discount the Gospel of John as a source for the life of the historical Jesus?

5. *Why do some scholars see Jesus as a teacher of wisdom rather than an apocalyptic prophet who predicted the end of the world? Which view of Jesus do you find more convincing and why?*

6. *What is the messianic secret? What is the evidence that there is a secret? Where is the secret broken? Is the secret a part of the life of the historical Jesus or is it, as Wrede argued, Mark's literary creation?*

7. *What is form criticism? Give two examples and propose a social context in the life of the early Christian community for the origin of your examples.*

8. *Describe redaction criticism and give two examples of two different literary forms that appear in both Matthew and Luke. Identify similarities and differences between the literary forms and their literary settings in the gospels. Account for the differences.*

9. *Describe the* Gospel of Thomas. *What is the evidence for its literary dependence or independence from the synoptic gospels? Give two examples showing the similarity and difference between the* Gospel of Thomas *and the canonical gospels. How do you account for this blend of similarity and difference?*

10. *What is the synoptic problem? Describe two different current solutions to the synoptic problem. How would each of these solutions affect a description of the historical Jesus?*

3

JESUS IN THE GOSPELS IN THE FIRST CENTURY

No uniform view of Jesus ever existed among his earliest followers or among others who knew him in the first century. The reports in the canonical gospels and noncanonical literature make this plain.[1] The gospels relate a variety of responses to him (see chart, p. 31 below).

The Talmud (*b. Sanh.* 43a) describes Jesus as a sorcerer and an apostate who deceived the Jewish people. Other Jewish sources claim he was the illegitimate child of Mary (*b. Šabb.* 104b).

What was important about Jesus in early Christian preaching and confession was his death and resurrection. Among his followers he was eulogized in confessional statements to the extent that his human life became relatively unimportant. Compare the following to see how his public life in Palestine was eclipsed in the confessions: Phil 2:5–11; 1 Tim 3:16; Heb 1:1–4; Col 1:15–20; Rom 1:1–4; John 1:1–18. Aspects of his public life, his deeds and words, are just barely retained in early Christian preaching as reported in Acts 1–12 (Acts 2:22; 10:34–39), and all details of his life are lacking in Acts 1:21–22 and 4:10.

In the latter half of the first century some gospel literature attempted to fill in these sketchy reminders of his public life. In one sense, the gospels might be seen as opposing a christological trend in the church that did not value his life. Nevertheless, as evidenced by the creeds that prevailed in the later centuries, the church continued to disregard his public career (his deeds and words) as significant for describing him. Leaping from his birth to his death and resurrection, early Christian writings virtually omit any reference to his life in the world.[2] The Apostles' Creed (ca. 340),[3] for example, reads: "I believe in God almighty and in Christ Jesus, his only son, our Lord, who was born of the Holy Spirit and the Virgin Mary, who was crucified under Pontius Pilate and was buried and the third day rose from the dead. . . ." The creed leaps from his miraculous birth to his death and resurrection: viz., "born of the Holy Spirit and the Virgin Mary . . . crucified[4] under Pontius Pilate."

GOSPEL PORTRAITS OF JESUS

	Matthew	Mark	Luke	John
He was accused of being demon possessed	9:34/12:24 10:25	3:22–23	11:15, 18–19	7:20 8:48–49, 52 10:20–21
he was thought to be insane		3:21		10:20
he was found to be socially deviant in that: (a) he associated with those outside the social boundaries of pious Jewish society	9:10–11 11:19	2:15–16	5:29–30 7:34 15:1–2 19:7	
(b) he was not strict in sabbath observance	12:1–8 12:9–14	2:23–28 3:1–6	6:1–5 6:6–11 13:10–17 14:1–6	5:1–16 9:1–16
(c) he did not observe ceremonial washing	15:1–20	7:1–23	11:37–41	

Early gospel literature, however, insists that the exalted Lord of early Christian faith was a man of humble Jewish origins whose personal identity was bound up in what he said and did. While his public life is portrayed in the gospels in somewhat larger than human dimensions, it is nevertheless recognizable as the life of a first-century Jewish man—even though the gospels do not always agree on the details.

Diversity—even contradiction—among the gospels should not be surprising. Should the situation with Jesus be any different than with anyone else? Are not all subject to what others think about us and how they perceive us? We have all experienced a certain surprise when we are forced, for whatever reason, to revise our faulty perceptions of others. There exist as many perceptions of each of us as there are people to perceive us. Even our own perceptions of ourselves constitute simply one view among many, and our own view may not be definitive for the way we will be remembered. Who among us can really claim to "know ourselves," as the philosophers advised?

The following are brief diverging "portraits"[5] of Jesus that can reasonably be inferred from the gospels of Mark, Matthew, Luke, John, and *Thomas*. Each presents a particular narrative description of aspects of the public life of Jesus. The portraits below deliberately draw on the distinctives of each gospel's presentation. Readers are cautioned that the "portrait" of any one gospel will likely not correspond completely to their own view. Most of us have preconceived views about Jesus that we inherited or borrowed from our church, parents, or televangelists. We might be tempted to judge an individual gospel portrait by the constructs we inherited or borrowed. For this chapter, however, readers are encouraged to shelve their preconceptions and engage each gospel as though they were hearing its story for the first time.

∞ MARK'S VIEW OF JESUS

Mark's opening words (1:1–12) describe Jesus as "Son of God" (1:1) and Lord (1:3). Mark says little about Jesus' origins, except that Nazareth may have been his family's village (1:24; 10:47; 14:67; 16:6). Jesus' mother's name was Mary; his four brothers were James, Joses, Judas, and Simon. Mark does not name his sisters. He was a carpenter by trade (6:3). He was baptized[6] by the "messenger" John (1:2–4), who preached a baptism of "repentance for the forgiveness of sins" (1:4)[7] and announced the coming of

Baptism

one who "would baptize with the Holy Spirit" (1:7–8). Mark does not explain why Jesus was baptized. Was he one of the masses (1:5) who went to the Jordan to be baptized by John? Did he, like they, confess his sins when he was baptized by John (1:9)? At his baptism the Spirit descended on him (1:10) and a heavenly voice addressed him as "my beloved son" (1:11).

Jesus proclaimed the nearness of the "kingdom of God" and called for "repentance and belief" in his "gospel of God," which he preached in view of the nearness of the kingdom (1:14–15). Mark, however, does not specify the nature of this kingdom. Jesus preached repentance, but he associated with tax collectors and sinners without demanding that they first repent (2:15–17).

He invited disciples, or students, to join him (1:16–17). In Galilee and Jericho Jesus (and his disciples to some degree; cf. 6:7, 12 to 9:18, 28–29) cast out demons (5:1–20; 7:24–30; 9:14–29), healed the sick and infirm (2:1–12; 5:24–34; 6:53–56), gave sight to the blind (8:22–26; 10:46–52) and hearing to the deaf (7:31–37), manipulated the forces of nature (4:35–41; 8:1–10), and cleansed lepers (1:40–45).[8] He sent out the "Twelve" (disciples) two-by-two on a preaching, exorcising, and healing mission (6:7–12, 30).

miracles

Jesus referred to himself as Son of Man, an obscure title Mark never clarified (2:10, 28; 8:38; 9:9, 12, 31; 13:26; 14:21, 41). Jesus claimed to have authority to forgive sins (2:10), yet he broke the rules of his own religious tradition (2:15–17; 3:1–6), as did his disciples (2:18, 23–24; 7:1–5). Because of this, the Jewish religious leaders conspired to kill him (3:6; 11:18; 12:12–13; 14:10–11, 43, 55, 64). When they asked him for a sign from heaven, he refused (8:11–13).

Parables[9] were Jesus' chief means of teaching and speaking to the crowds (4:33–34). The purpose of these obscure stories was to keep people from understanding him, because if they understood him they might repent and be forgiven (4:10–12). The secret about the kingdom of God contained in the stories was meant only for disciples. Hence Jesus usually explained his teachings to them away from the crowds (4:10, 34; 9:28). Yet even his disciples failed to understand (4:40; 6:52; 8:14–21, 31–33; 9:9–13, 32).

parables

Jesus apparently did not want his identity as "God's son" and Messiah known, and he tried to keep it a secret from the masses. He silenced the demons that he exorcised (1:34; 3:11–12) and commanded those he healed not to reveal his identity (1:43–44; 5:43; 7:36; cf. 8:26). He even directed his disciples not to betray his identity (8:29–30; 9:9). But despite his efforts the "secret" was not completely kept (1:44–45). Perhaps it was because Jesus was not always consistent in his instructions (5:19–20; 14:61–62).

He preached primarily in Galilee and Judea, although he once visited the tetrarchy of Philip (5:1–20), Syria and the Decapolis (7:24–31), and made one trip to Judea (Mark 10–16). That Jesus restricted his preaching principally to Jewish territory and only rarely healed those outside Judaism (the Greek woman's daughter, 7:24–30) suggest that he understood his mission to be directed primarily to his own Jewish people.

Whatever else the term Son of Man may have signified to Mark, it clearly meant that Jesus' mission would end in suffering and death. Jesus understood the significance of his death to be "a ransom for many" (10:45), but Mark never clarifies precisely what that means. Jesus openly predicted his rejection by the Jewish religious authorities, his death, and his resurrection from the dead after three days (8:31; 9:30–32; 10:32–34). Jesus believed that the kingdom of God was appearing in his day; there is a sense of immediacy in the way he described its nearness (1:15). Apparently his mighty deeds of healing (5:25–34), exorcising of demons (5:1–20), and manipulation of nature (6:30–44) were signs of its immediate appearing (3:22–27; in particular 3:27: Jesus is the one who "binds the strong man"). His opponents, however, regarded these signs as evidence of his collusion with Satan. He announced that some of those who heard him preach would not die until they saw "that the kingdom of God has come with power" (9:1).

He called on his disciples to become servants of all (9:35; 10:43–44), and to cut off hands and feet or pluck out an eye, if these caused them to sin (9:43–47). He strictly prohibited divorce (10:1–12), even though it was permitted by the Scripture (Deut 24:1–4). He called for his disciples to divest themselves of material wealth (10:17–22), since it was not possible for a rich person to enter the kingdom of God (10:23–27). He instructed his students to follow him as wandering beggars (10:21–22; cf. 6:8–11). To those who followed him in this mendicant mission he promised eternal life (10:30), "treasure in heaven" (10:21), and also "now in this life" a hundred times more than what they had given up to follow him (10:28–30). He apparently believed that his disciples merely had to ask God in order to receive what they wanted (11:22–24).

He drove the merchants out of the temple and overturned the tables of the money changers, accusing them of turning a "house of prayer" into a "den of thieves" (11:15–19). This deed, coupled with criticism of the religious leaders of Judaism (11:27–12:12), prompted his death (12:12). During his last days, he celebrated the traditional Jewish Passover with his disciples (14:1–2, 12–25), and he predicted that Peter would deny him: "This very night before the cock crows twice, you will deny me three times" (14:30). When death was imminent, he tried to avoid it, but ultimately resigned himself to the inevitable (14:32–42). He was betrayed by Judas, one of his followers (14:10–11), and was arrested (14:43–48). He was taken before Jewish (14:53–72) and Roman (15:1–20) officials before he was crucified (15:21–39). His last words from the cross were, "My God, my God, why have you forsaken me?" (15:34). He was buried by Joseph, a member of the Jewish council (15:42–47). When his women followers (15:40–41) went to the tomb early on the first day of the week (Mary Magdalene and Mary the mother of James and Salome, 16:1) after the sabbath had passed (16:1–2), they found the tomb empty (16:3–8). A young man inside the tomb told them to go to Galilee where they would see Jesus (16:7; cf. 9:9; 14:28). But in fear they failed to tell anyone anything (16:8).[10] Since the narrative refers only to one Passover, a reader might reasonably infer that the public career of Jesus lasted one year or less.

∞ MATTHEW'S VIEW OF JESUS

Matthew described Jesus as the virgin-born son of Mary (1:18–25), but traced his family line through Mary's husband Joseph (1:16), the carpenter (13:55), to King David (1:6) and even back to Abraham (1:1), the patriarch of Hebrew faith. Matthew asserted that events in Jesus' life happened "in order to fulfill what was spoken by the prophets" (1:22–23; 2:5–6, 15, 17–18, 23; 3:3; 4:14–16; 8:17; 12:17–21; 13:14–15, 35; 21:4–5). Jesus was born in Bethlehem in Judea sometime before the death of Herod the king (in 4 B.C.E.) (2:1). His birth, apparently in a house in Bethlehem

(2:11), was heralded by heavenly portents and was revered by astrologers from the East (2:1–2). While he was still a child (2:16) his family moved to Nazareth to avoid Archelaus, who was ethnarch of Judea and Herod's son (2:19–23). Jesus had sisters, and four brothers named James, Joseph, Simon, and Judas (13:55–56).

Jesus was one of the multitudes who came to John in the wilderness (3:1–6) for baptism (3:13). John preached a baptism of repentance for those who confessed their sins (3:5–6, 11) and also announced the coming of one who "would baptize with the Holy Spirit and fire" (3:11). John at first refused to baptize Jesus, declining because of his own feelings of unworthiness (3:14); but Jesus insisted, because in that way "righteousness was fulfilled" (3:15). At Jesus' baptism by John, the Spirit of God descended on Jesus (3:16) and a heavenly voice proclaimed to the crowds: "This is my beloved son" (3:17). In a contest with the devil he demonstrated his knowledge of Torah and his superiority over the devil (4:1–11) before he began his public career. When he heard that John had been arrested, Jesus went to Capernaum in Galilee (4:12–13) and began preaching. He demanded repentance in view of the immediate coming of the kingdom of heaven (4:17). He proclaimed that some of those who heard him preach would not die before they saw "the Son of Man come in his kingdom" (16:28). Son of Man is an obscure title that Jesus apparently used for himself (16:13–15).

He called disciples (4:18–22; 10:1–4) and traveled throughout Galilee teaching, preaching, healing, and exorcising demons (4:23–25). He claimed that his exorcisms signaled the presence of God's kingdom (12:28), but the Jewish religious leaders accused him of casting out demons by demonic powers (12:24–32). Although he healed the sick (8:5–17; 9:1–8, 20–22, 27–31, 35–38; 11:2–6; 20:29–34), cured lepers (8:1–4), exorcised demons (8:28–34; 9:32–34; 12:22–23), demonstrated his power over nature (8:23–27; 14:13–33; 15:32–39), and even raised the dead (9:18–19, 23–26), the hallmark of his career was teaching the crowds that came out to hear him (Matt 5–7; 10:5–42), principally using parables (13:1–52) about the kingdom of heaven. But, according to Matthew, people simply refused to understand what he was trying to teach them with the parables, because they had deliberately hardened their hearts against what he taught (13:10–17).

Jesus preached repentance in view of the coming kingdom of heaven (4:17) but associated with tax collectors and sinners without demanding that they first repent (9:10–13). His disciples were lax in observing Jewish religious traditions. They did not fast (9:14–17) and violated sabbath laws (12:1–8), as did Jesus himself (12:9–13). Jesus actually publicly contrasted his views with Scripture (5:21–22, 27–28, 31–32, 33–36, 38–39, 43–44), although he believed that Torah would always be obligatory (5:17–19). According to Jesus, all the obligations of Torah and the Prophets (divisions of the sacred writings of Israel) could be fulfilled by simply loving God and one's neighbor (22:34–40). He stated that his mission was to Israel only (15:24), although he did consent to heal a Roman centurion's servant (8:5–13) and a Canaanite woman's daughter (15:21–28). His opponents were the Jewish religious leaders: Pharisees (23:1–39), Sadducees (16:1, 11–12; 19:3; 22:15), Herodians, priests, and scribes (21:14–16), and he criticized them severely (Matt 23). When his opponents demanded a sign, he gave them the sign of Jonah (16:1–4) and explained that it referred to two things: his own resurrection (12:38–40) and the repentance of the masses at his preaching (12:41).

He sent twelve of his disciples to the "lost sheep of the house of Israel," commissioning them to proclaim the imminence of the kingdom of heaven and to heal the sick, raise the dead, cleanse lepers, and exorcise demons (10:5–8). There is no evidence that they actually succeeded, only that they failed when they tried (17:14–21)—although Jesus believed that nothing was impossible for them (17:20).

His disciples believed that he was the Messiah, Son of the living God (16:13–17), and this was apparently generally known (2:1–12), although there were some things that Jesus did not want to become public knowledge (9:30–31; 17:9). On three occasions he told his disciples he would be killed and raised on the third day after his death (16:21; 17:22–23; 20:17–19). Jesus intended to establish a "church" (or "assembly," ἐκκλησία, 16:18–20), and gave instructions for church governance (5:21–26; 18:15–22). He gave specific instructions how his followers should comport their lives (Matt 5–7). To Peter he gave the "keys of the kingdom of heaven" for binding and loosing things in heaven and on earth (16:18–20).

He taught his followers that with one exception divorce was not permitted: a man may divorce his wife if she had been unfaithful to him (5:31–32; 19:3–9). He taught them not to resist an evil person, and always to give to beggars and borrowers (5:38–42). They should not disfigure their faces when they were fasting (6:16–18). They should not judge others (7:1–5) and should have a forgiving spirit (6:14–15), for they would be judged as they judged, and be forgiven as they forgave. With a model prayer he taught them how to pray (6:9–13) and urged them always to pray in secret rather than publicly (6:5–6).

He called on his disciples to become servants (20:25–28; 23:10–12) and to give away all their earthly possessions to the poor (19:16–22), for wealth will keep a rich man from entering the kingdom of heaven (19:23–26). For the sake of the kingdom of heaven some men will even be called upon to make themselves eunuchs (19:12).[11] For these acts of impoverishment and self-denial they would be compensated a hundred times over for what they had given up and would inherit eternal life (19:25–30).

He created a disturbance of the peace in the temple, overturning the tables of the money changers, driving out the merchants (21:12–13), and publicly censuring the religious leaders of Judaism (21:23–27, 33–46; ch. 23). For these actions and others, the religious leaders plotted his death (12:14; 21:45–46; 26:3–5). Eventually he was betrayed by one of his own followers for thirty pieces of silver (26:14–16, 45–47). Judas, the betrayer, eventually hanged himself in despair (27:3–10).

During his last days, Jesus celebrated the traditional Jewish Passover with his disciples (26:17–29). On that occasion he predicted that Peter, one of his disciples, would deny him: "This very night before the cock crows you will deny me three times" (26:34). When the authorities came to arrest him, his disciples tried to defend him with a sword, but he told them not to do so, for "all who take the sword will perish by the sword" (26:47–54). He appeared before both Jewish (26:57–75) and Roman (27:1–26) officials, and as a result was crucified (27:33–54). His last words from the cross were, "My God, my God, why have you forsaken me?" (27:46). At his death there was a great earthquake, tombs were opened, and many dead "saints" were raised and appeared in Jerusalem (27:51–53). Joseph, a wealthy man

Death

of Arimathea, claimed his body, burying it in Joseph's own new tomb (27:57–61). When Jesus' women followers (27:55–56) went to the tomb toward the dawn of the first day of the week (Mary Magdalene and the other Mary, 28:1), they found an angel of the Lord sitting outside the tomb—even the guards at the tomb were shocked (28:2–4). The angel told them to go to Galilee where they would see him (28:5–7). The women ran to tell the disciples and met Jesus on the way (28:8–10). Later the disciples gathered in Galilee and Jesus appeared to them telling them to "Go and make disciples of all nations, baptizing them in the name of the Father, Son and Holy Spirit" (28:16–20). Since there is only one Passover mentioned in the narrative, a reader would reasonably infer that the public career of Jesus lasted one year or less.

ɷɷ Luke's View of Jesus

The prologue by Luke suggests that previous narratives about Jesus were deficient in some way but that Luke's narrative sets out a correct version of those events with eyewitness information (1:1–4). The story begins with Jesus' birth preceded by that of his kinsman (1:34–36) John (1:57–66). John's birth (1:8–23), like Jesus' own birth (1:26–35), was announced by an angel prior to conception (John, 1:24; Jesus, 1:31). John was the prophet of the Most High (1:13–17, 67–79), whose mission was to prepare people for the coming of the Son of God (1:76–79). Jesus was that promised Son of God (1:32–36). A heavenly choir announced Jesus' birth to lowly shepherds (2:8–14) when he was born to a virgin named Mary (1:26–27) in Bethlehem (2:4). She laid her infant son in a cattle feeding box (2:16) in a stable (2:7) during a Roman census (2:1–2), taken when Quirinius was governor of Syria (6–7 C.E.). Jesus was circumcised on the eighth day (2:21) following his birth, as the Torah prescribed (Gen 17:12), as was also his kinsman John (1:59). Proper sacrifices were made in the temple after Mary completed her purification following childbirth (2:22–24; cf. Lev 12:2–8). As a child Jesus astounded the teachers of Judaism in Jerusalem with his knowledge (2:41–51).

John preached (3:1–9) and performed (3:10–14) a baptism of repentance for the forgiveness of sins. He announced the coming of one who "would baptize with the Holy Spirit and fire" (3:15–16). John criticized the actions of the political ruler of Galilee and as a result was thrown into prison (3:18–20). Immediately after John was imprisoned, Jesus was baptized in the Jordan. The Holy Spirit then descended on him and a heavenly voice addressed him as "my beloved son" (3:21–22). Luke traces Jesus' genealogy through his stepfather[12] Joseph back to Adam, the first human—and even back to God himself (3:23–38). Full of the Holy Spirit, Jesus undergoes a period of testing in the wilderness, during which he defeated the devil (4:1–12), who then leaves him alone "until an opportune time" (4:13). At about thirty years of age (3:23) Jesus began preaching in Galilee in the power of the Spirit (4:14–15). He announced in the village of Nazareth, the hometown of his stepfather Joseph (2:4), that his work gave priority to the Gentiles (4:22–30). When asked, he said that his marvelous deeds affirmed him as the "one who is to come" (7:18–35). And hence his career was accompanied by exorcisms of demons (4:31–37; 6:17–19; 8:1–3, 26–39; 9:37–43), raising the dead (7:11–16, 8:49–56), the healing of lepers (5:12–16; 17:11–19) and the sick (4:38–41; 8:42–48; 18:35–43). He performed deeds that demonstrated his power over nature (8:22–25; 9:10–17), and even forgave sins (7:36–50). The message he preached was the "good news of the kingdom of God" (4:42–44).

Jesus called disciples (6:12–16) to follow him and become "fishers of men" (5:1–11), and they left everything to follow him on his itinerant preaching mission (5:11, 27–28). Some of his close followers were women who supported his ministry financially (8:1–3; 23:55). He commissioned twelve of his disciples to go on a mission of exorcising, preaching, and healing (9:1–6). Later, he commissioned another seventy disciples for a second similar mission, sending them out two by two (10:1–20).

He argued with the Pharisees and teachers of Torah (5:17–26; 6:1–11; 11:42–54), the chief priests, and the scribes (20:1–47) over his career of teaching, healing, and exorcising demons. They accused him of performing exorcisms by the power of the prince of demons (11:14–23). But he claimed that the kingdom of God was present in the world (17:20–21), and that his deeds provided evidence that it was present (11:20). He associated with toll collectors and sinners for the purpose of calling them to repentance (5:29–32). He had come specifically to call such people, rather than the righteous (5:32).

He claimed that the kingdom of God belonged to poor people (6:20). In the future there would be a reversal of fortunes: those who currently lacked and suffered would be blessed (6:21–23; 14:12–24). Conversely the rich would be disenfranchised (6:24–26). Indeed it was his opinion that wealth will keep a rich person from entering the kingdom of God (18:18–30; cf. 21:1–4). But those who leave everything behind to follow him will be more than compensated in this life, and in the age to come they will receive eternal life (18:29–30). He called for love of enemies and nonviolence (6:27–36). He taught that God judges on the basis of how one treats others (6:37–42).

Much of his teaching was in parables (8:4–18; 10:29–37; 13:1–9, 18–21; 14:15–33; 15:1–32; 16:1–13; 18:1–14; 19:11–27; 20:9–18). Explanations were intended only for the disciples, however. Jesus did not want the masses to understand his parables (8:9–10). He predicted that he would be killed and raised on the third day (9:18–22, 43–45; 18:31–34), and he called on his followers to imitate his example (9:23–25).When the time for his death drew near, he resolutely turned toward Jerusalem, continuing his career of teaching, healing, and exorcising as he traveled (9:51–19:44). *Parables*

He drove merchants out of the temple, because he thought the temple should be a "house of prayer" (19:45–46), and this act led to the conspiracy to kill him (6:1–11; 19:47–48; 20:19). One of his own followers, Judas, betrayed him (22:3–6, 47–48). He also predicted that another would deny him: "Peter, the cock will not crow this day before you deny me three times" (22:34, 60–62). At his arrest he reversed earlier instructions (22:35–36; cf. 10:4) he had given to the disciples and told them they now needed a sword (22:36–38).

Before his death he ate the traditional Passover meal with his disciples (22:7–23) and resigned himself to his inevitable death (22:39–46). He appeared before Jewish religious leaders (22:54–71), a Roman official (23:1–25), and also before the Jewish civil authority of Galilee (23:6–12). His last words from the cross were, "Father into thy hands I commit my spirit" (23:46). His women followers went to the tomb at daybreak on the first day of the week (they were Mary Magdalene, Joanna, Mary the mother of James, and certain other women, 24:10). They found the stone rolled away and, entering, they found the tomb empty (24:1–2). In the tomb two men in dazzling apparel told them to go and tell the disciples, but the disciples did not believe the women (24:4–12). Later Jesus appeared to his disciples and commanded them to remain in Jerusalem (24:49) until they were endowed with divine power (24:49). The mention of one Passover in the narrative suggests that the public career of Jesus lasted one year or less.

∞ JOHN'S VIEW OF JESUS

In a prologue (1:1–18) the author describes Jesus as the preexistent Son of God, the agent through whom all creation came into existence. He became flesh and dwelt in the world as one full of the grace, truth, and glory of God. People neither recognized nor welcomed him. Jesus was the one who rested in the Father's bosom and revealed the Father (1:1–5, 9–14, 16–17). John the baptizer testified that Jesus had brought light into the world (1:6–8, 15, 23–27), and also claimed he saw the Spirit descend on Jesus (1:29–32). He publicly proclaimed Jesus as the Son of God, who would baptize others with the Holy Spirit (1:33–34; 3:27–30). John the Baptist's public career overlapped that of Jesus (3:22–24). Both Jesus and his disciples (1:29–51) baptized others into their company (3:22; but cf. 4:2), at the same time (3:23–24) John was baptizing.

Jesus' identity as Son of God and king of Israel was not a secret (1:29, 34, 36, 41, 49). He referred to himself by the obscure and enigmatic title "Son of Man," which the author of John does not clarify (1:51; 3:13–14; 5:27; 6:27, 53, 62; 8:28; 12:23, 34; 13:31). His public career was characterized by miraculous deeds, which the writer refers to as "signs" that reveal his glory and produce faith in people who observe them (2:11, 18, 23; 3:2; 4:54; 6:14, 26, 30; 10:41–42; 11:45–48; 12:36–43; 20:30–31). Although Jesus did not claim to have the authority to forgive sins, and did not condemn sinners (5:14; 16:7–11), he gave his disciples such authority (20:22–23).

He did not speak in parables, but instead used cryptic language[13] and obscure sayings that puzzled his hearers (10:1–6;
11:5–16; 16:16–19). He typically spoke in long discourses (5:19–47;
10:1–18; 12:44–50; 15:1–16:16; 17:1–26). Even when he was simply
talking with others, he tended to deliver short "speeches" (6:1–71;
7:14–44; 8:12–58; 10:22–39; 12:20–36; 14:1–31; 16:16–33). His language included such unusual expressions as:

- I am the bread of life (6:35, 48)
- unless you eat the flesh of the
  Son of Man and drink his blood
  you will not have eternal life (6:53–54)
- I am the door of the sheep (10:7)
- I am the door (10:9)
- I am the good shepherd (10:11)

- I am the way, the truth, and the life (14:6)
- I am the resurrection and the life (11:25)
- I am the true vine (15:1)
- I am the light of the world (8:12; 9:5).

His signs included turning water to wine (2:1–11), healing the
sick (4:46–54; 5:2–15), miraculously feeding five thousand (6:1–14),
giving sight to the blind (9:1–41), and raising the dead (11:1–45).
But he performed no exorcisms. Early in his career he drove merchants and money changers out of the temple with a scourge
(2:13–20), but his opponents were bothered more by his breaking
sabbath restrictions, his making himself equal with God (5:16–18),
and his signs (11:45–53) than they were by his disrupting the
temple. And for these reasons they plotted to kill him (5:18; 11:53).
While his opponents included Pharisees and chief priests (4:1;
7:32, 45; 9:40; 11:45–53), throughout the gospel his opponents are
primarily described as "the Jews" (passim).

He scarcely mentions the kingdom of God (3:3, 5; cf. 18:35);
hence the kingdom of God is not the focus of his preaching. God's
judgment seems to occur at the moment a person believes in Jesus
(3:16–21). Jesus does expect a future end to the world, but this expectation plays only a minimal role in his preaching (6:39–40, 44,
54), and hence he does not warn people of the nearness of the end.
The substance of his message is that he alone brings eternal life
(3:15–21; 4:7–26; 5:24, 30–47; 6:35–40, 50–51; 8:13–19; 10:16–18,
25–30, 34–38; 11:25–26; 12:44–50; 14:6–14; 15:1–11; 17:1–26).

At the end of his career he celebrated a final meal with his disciples shortly before the Jewish Passover (13:1; 19:14, 31, 42) during which he washed their feet and directed that they should
continue the practice (13:1–15). He was betrayed by a disciple

named Judas (6:70–71; 13:2, 21–30; 18:2–5). Jesus had predicted that another disciple, Peter, would deny him three times "before the cock crowed" (13:38), and so it happened (18:17, 25–27). He was taken before both Jewish (18:12–24) and Roman (18:28–19:16) officials before being crucified. He was forced to carry his own cross (19:17) to the place he was crucified (19:18–30). His last words from the cross were "It is finished" (19:30). He died before the Passover and was buried on the day of preparation for the Passover meal (19:42). His body was given to Joseph of Arimathea, a disciple of Jesus, who buried him in a new garden tomb (19:38–42). Mary Magdalene went to the tomb on the first day of the week and found it empty. She immediately told Peter and another disciple, and both went to the tomb. They saw only the empty graveclothes (20:4–8). When Mary looked into the tomb later, she saw two angels in white sitting where the body of Jesus had been. Later she saw the resurrected Lord outside the tomb (20:1–17) and told the disciples (20:18). Subsequently Jesus appeared twice, once in Jerusalem and once in Galilee (20:19–21:23). John's gospel describes the significance of Jesus' crucifixion as his moment of glorification that brings the defeat of the world ruler (7:39; 11:4; 12:16, 23, 28; 12:27–33; 13:31–32; 14:30; 17:1–5). Because John's gospel mentions three Passovers (2:13; 11:55; 18:28), a reader might reasonably infer Jesus' public career lasted about three years.

 JESUS IN THE *GOSPEL OF THOMAS*

The *Gospel of Thomas* is not a narrative gospel like Matthew, Mark, Luke, and John, but is instead a sayings gospel. It tells no story but is comprised simply of a collection of sayings attributed to "the living Jesus" (prologue).[14] The "living Jesus" is the "son of the living one" (37:3; cf. 37:59) and he proclaims the "living Father" (3:4; 15; 37:3; 50:2; 52:2; 111:2). He comes from beyond this world (28:1–4), from "that which is whole" (61:3). He claims to be the "All," and as such is the light over everything (77). His true identity, however, is unknown (13; 43; 61; 91).

He announces that the "kingdom" of the Father is present (3:1–3; 46:2; 49; 54; 113) in him (82), and thus he rejects future apocalyptic (cosmic) expectations (18; 51). He speaks Wisdom's message (Wis 7:27–28; 10:16) in banal or community wisdom (i.e., in proverbs: 33:2–3; 35; 45; 47), in double-edged and subversive aphorisms (3:4–5; 5; 7; 10; 14:5; 17; 22:4–7; 25:1–2; 26; 31; 34; 56; 61:5; 89; 93; 108), in parables (8; 9; 20; 57; 63; 64; 65; 76; 96; 97; 98; 107; 109), and in paradoxes (55; 101; 105), but he never bothers to explain his discourse (prologue; 1). Rather, those who find the interpretation of these sayings will live forever (1; 2; 18; 19), for the "living" do not die (11:2; 58; 84) since they live in the living one (111:2; cf. 4:1).

Although he "calls" (90), and people follow him as disciples (6:1; 12:1; 13:1; 19:2; 21:1; 22:1–2; 61:4), he is not a teacher (13:5). He prefers a neutral term like "leader" (12), but rejects all attempts to categorize him in terms of popular expectations (13). His followers are to become "like him" to such an extent that they and he become one (108). He claims that wisdom cannot "be taught"; people must intuit wisdom (2; 3:5; 18; 24; 46:2; 62; 70; 91:2; 92:1; 94; 108; 111:3). They do this by becoming solitary wanderers (16:4; 42; 49) and by being poor, persecuted, and hungry (54; 68; 69; 81). Hence his followers are to reject the world (110), the marketplace (64:12), and wealth (95; but cf. 109). They should expect the world to be a place of trouble because of their radical lifestyle (10; 16). Jesus disavows traditional religious piety such as fasting, prayer, ritual, and almsgiving (6; 14; 39; 53; 89; 102; but cf. 27 and 104), as well as normal community obligations (55; 101; 105).

To those who follow him he offers disturbance and rest (2:2–3; 50:3; 51:1; 60:6; 90), immortality/eternal life (1; 18; 19), a shared reign over the All (2), and fullness or fulfillment—that is to say, their lack/poverty will be filled with "wealth" (3:5; 28; 29; 54). Those who find the interpretation of his words will achieve the perfect androgynous state of the original human being, Adam (18:2; 22:4–7; 50; 114; cf. Gen 2:21–25), and that final state will be greater than the original state of humanity (85), for the end is greater than the beginning (18:3).

∞

These brief contrasting descriptions of Jesus from the five gospels show that he was viewed differently in early Christian tradition. The differences expose the distinctives of each writer's perception of Jesus. A close comparative reading of the texts will reveal other differences and similarities. There are a number of reasons for the differences: each writer had different information available; each author chose different material to draft the narrative; the authors held unique religious views; and each author wrote for a particular social and religious situation. A great deal of similarity also exists in content and in the sequence of material, particularly among Matthew, Mark, and Luke. The similarities and differences among the gospels will be taken up in detail in the next chapter. At this point, however, three of the descriptions (Matthew, Mark, and Luke) are clearly quite similar, while the other two descriptions are quite different. One is different in terms of its content and form (*Thomas*, a sayings gospel); the other (John) in terms of the sequence of events and the rather different way Jesus' career is presented.

⅋ RECOMMENDED READING AND SOURCES CONSULTED

It is difficult to find readings that either (a) do not harmonize the gospels into one, uniform description of Jesus, or (b) do not initially assume a particular solution to explain the different descriptions of Jesus in the gospels.

BORG, MARCUS J. *Meeting Jesus Again for the First Time: The Historical Jesus and the Heart of Contemporary Faith.* San Francisco: HarperSanFrancisco, 1994. DAVIES, STEVAN. *The Gospel of Thomas and Christian Wisdom.* New York: Seabury, 1983. Pages 36–99. HARRIS, STEPHEN L. *The New Testament: A Student's Introduction.* 2d ed. Mountain View, Calif.: Mayfield, 1995. Pages 66–189. MAYS, J. L. *Interpreting the Gospels.* Philadelphia: Fortress, 1981. Pages 55–96, 115–29, 148–67, 183–213, 278–90. SPIVEY, R. A., and D. M. SMITH. *Anatomy of the New Testament: A Guide to Its Structure and Meaning.* 4th ed. New York: Macmillan, 1989. Pages 65–189. STANTON, G. N. *The Gospels and Jesus.* Oxford: Oxford University Press, 1989. Pages 34–124.

⅋ ISSUES FOR STUDY AND DISCUSSION

1. *Compare the presentations of Jesus in Mark and John described above. What similarities and differences do you notice? Suggest plausible reasons for the diversity.*

2. Compare Matthew, Mark, and Luke for their similarities and differences. Explain this blend of close similarity and striking difference.

3. Which of the canonical gospels is the Gospel of Thomas *most like? Why do you suppose the* Gospel of Thomas *is so different from the other four?*

4. Which of the five narratives is your own view of Jesus most like? Unlike? From what do you suppose your own view of Jesus likely derives? What assumptions about the gospel literature could have led you to understand Jesus as you do?

5. What features in the above descriptions of Jesus do you find objectionable? To what do you attribute these features? Were they actually historical aspects of Jesus' life? Why, or why not?

6. How do you suppose these different portraits among the gospels can be accommodated into a consistent description of Jesus of Nazareth? Is such a construction possible? Why, or why not?

7. Can you write a description of Jesus that would accommodate the similarity and differences among the following?

a. Mark and John
b. Matthew, Mark, and Luke
c. Mark and Gospel of Thomas
d. John and Gospel of Thomas
e. Gospel of Thomas, *and either Matthew or Luke*

8. Which gospel do you find most believable as a historical narrative? Why? Whose do you find least believable as a historical narrative? Why?

9. Should one give a preference to the canonical gospels over the Gospel of Thomas? *Why or why not? What is the value of the* Gospel of Thomas?

10. Do you disagree with any of the descriptions of Jesus above? Using the same format, write your own brief description of Jesus from that gospel.

4

DIVERSITY AMONG THE GOSPELS

This chapter examines the diversity between the narratives of the synoptic gospels (using Mark as an example) and the Gospel of John. It will also explore differences and similarities among the synoptic gospels, Matthew, Mark, and Luke. Before proceeding, however, it is important to note that the frequently profound differences in how the gospel writers recount what appear to be identical events in the public career of Jesus often surprise and disturb readers who have never looked closely, or with a critical eye, at the New Testament. For those of us who have grown up reading the New Testament as unique sacred literature, the anxiety can be very real. Often our first response might be to question why we were never better informed about the diversity among the gospel writings. Or we might be pressed to ask whether, if the diversity is present, the gospels can truly be without error, disagreement, or discord. Do inconsistencies in writings that should be in perfect harmony with each other, at least according to some belief systems, collide with a faith commitment that the writings are "inspired"? Unless we ask such questions and explore genuine resolutions to such issues, we will be responding only with a view toward reconciling the passages in question with a prior confessed belief in the nature of the writings.[1] If we truly want to understand the literary and theological distinctives of each gospel, maintaining a prior commitment to the nature of the Bible must take a back seat. This does not mean abandoning faith, but it does require an accommodation of faith to the examination of the gospels with a fresh eye. To examine the gospels critically we may find it profitable to set aside our presuppositions as to the nature of the Bible in order to hear more clearly the voice of the gospels themselves. This will allow us to develop our own theories to explain their diversity and similarity.

Below we will compare the diversity among the narratives of the synoptic gospels and John. For several reasons, we will use Mark's gospel as a representative of the synoptics. First, because Mark is the shortest gospel, it is the easiest to compare. Second, Mark is generally regarded as the earliest of the synoptic gospels and a source for the other two. Third, Mark exhibits the closest narrative parallels with John. Fourth, Mark is generally regarded as the least theologically sophisticated, whereas John is held to be the most theologically advanced. For these reasons, the contrast between the two will be greater and thus the differences easier to see. Finally we will compare and contrast selected passages from the gospels of Matthew, Mark, and Luke. This will involve noting similarities and differences among the narratives, as well as examining how the writers narrate identical stories and sayings.

∞ VARIETY IN THE GOSPELS OF MARK AND JOHN

Mark and John describe Jesus in two remarkably different ways. In general they do not report the same incidents, and when they do overlap they are rather distinct. Their respective portraits of Jesus reflect few similarities, they structure Jesus' activities differently, and the cultural spirits of their books contrast sharply. Mark's Jesus moves comfortably in a world easily recognizable as traditionally Jewish. John's description of Jesus, on the other hand, has been more heavily influenced by the broader

Greco-Roman world of the day.[2] The debate continues and no consensus has emerged, but one may safely say that in its cultural outlook John more closely resembles the thought worlds of the Dead Sea Scrolls, Gnosticism, and Hermeticism than that of the Gospel of Mark.[3]

The contrasts between Mark and John can be classified as follows: variety in sequencing and structuring of events, variety in the character and style of Jesus' ministry, and differences in the content of specific events.

Variety in the Sequencing and Structuring of Events

Mark	John
1. Jesus begins his public career after John has been put into prison (1:14–15).	The public careers of Jesus and John run concurrently (3:22–24).
2. The cleansing of the temple occurs toward the conclusion of Jesus' career (11:15–19) and prompts the religious authorities to decide to kill him (11:18; cf. 3:6; 14:1).	The temple cleansing occurs at the beginning of the public career of Jesus (2:13–25), and his opponents do not plot to kill him until later, and not because of his disturbance in the temple (5:18; 8:37; 10:33; cf. 7:19–20; 11:53; 12:10–11).
3. The public career of Jesus is approximately one year or less—because the narrative mentions only one Passover celebration (chs. 14–16).	His career is approximately three years—because there are three Passover celebrations mentioned (2:13; 11:55; 18:28).
4. The public career of Jesus occurs in Galilee (and environs: chs. 1–9). He makes one trip to Jerusalem during his public career (10:1, 17, 32, 46; 11:1, 11), and is crucified (chs. 11–16).	There are five trips to Jerusalem (2:13, 23; 5:1; 7:10; 11:7, 18; 12:12); Jesus' public career incorporated both Galilee and Judea.
5. The last meal that Jesus has with his disciples is a traditional Passover celebration (14:1, 12, 17). Jesus is crucified the day after Passover, is buried the day before the Sabbath (15:42; 16:1–2), and is resurrected the day after the Sabbath.	The final meal Jesus celebrates with his disciples takes place before Passover (13:1, 18:28). Jesus is even crucified and buried on the day before Passover (19:14, 31, 42).

Variation in the Style and Character of Jesus' Ministry

Mark	John
1. Jesus is portrayed as attempting to keep his identity from becoming widely known. He silences the demons he exorcises to keep them from revealing his identity as the Son of God (1:24–25, 34, 3:11–12). He also silences those that he heals, apparently so that his activities will not become public knowledge (1:43–45, 5:43; 7:36; 8:26). He even tries to keep his disciples from revealing his identity (8:30; 9:9). But the secret is poorly kept and leaks out (1:44–45; 7:36). It is not until the end of his career that Jesus publicly acknowledges his identity (14:61–62).	Both his identity as the Son of God and his healing activities are generally known (1:29–34, 36, 41, 45, 49; 3:2; 4:25; 5:16–18; 6:29, 41–42, 68–70; 8:40–44; 9:11, 35–38; 10:19–21, 24–26, 40–42; 11:21–27; but cf. 7:25–27; 10:24).
2. Jesus performed a ministry of "mighty deeds" (δύναμις) that required faith before the deed could be performed (3:5; 5:6–8, 25–29, 36–42; 6:5–6, 56; 8:22–25; 9:14–27; 10:46–52; in the following, faith seems to be assumed: 1:29–34, 40–42; 3:10; 7:32–35).[4]	Jesus performs "signs" (σημεῖον) that produce faith in those who observe them (2:11, 23; 3:2; 4:45, 48, 54; 6:2, 14, 26, 30; 7:31; 9:35–38; 10:41–42; 11:45–48; 12:10–11, 18–19, 37; 20:30–31).
3. Exorcisms that Jesus performs are a demonstration of the presence and power of the kingdom of God (1:14–15; 3:21–27).[5]	No exorcisms appear in John.
4. What Jesus preached is summarized as the announcement of the nearness of the kingdom of God (1:14–15; 9:1), and throughout the short year of his career he focused on the kingdom in his preaching (4:11, 26; 9:47; 10:14–15, 23–25; 12:34; 14:25).	The kingdom is not a significant part of the preaching of Jesus. The word occurs five times in John's narrative, isolated to the Nicodemus story (3:3, 5) and Jesus' appearance before Pilate (18:36). The focus of Jesus' preaching in John is himself.
5. Jesus' characteristic form of address is the "parable." Mark says (4:33–34) Jesus only addressed the crowds in parables (παραβολή). Jesus did this because the kingdom was intended for the disciples and other insiders. Hence Jesus used parables with the crowds specifically to keep them from understanding; had they understood, they might repent and be forgiven (4:11–12).	There are no "parables" like the stories Jesus told in the synoptics. The word "parable" does not even appear in John. Instead Jesus uses the "riddle" (παροιμία), a type of obscure or unclear figurative language (10:1–5; 16:25–29).

6. Jesus speaks in brief memorable statements such as parables, aphorisms, and proverbs.

Jesus makes "speeches" (5:19–47; 10:1–18; 12:44–50; 15:1–16:16; 17:1–26); and even in his conversation he tends to use speeches (6:1–71; 8:12–58; 14:1–31).

7. Jesus' principal enemies are the Pharisees, Herodians, Sadducees, scribes, chief priests, and the elders (2:16; 3:6; 7:1; 8:11; 10:2; 11:27; 12:13, 18, 28, 32; 14:43, 53; 15:1).

Jesus' enemies are primarily "the Jews," or perhaps better the "Judaites" (Ἰουδαῖοι). The Pharisees (1:24; 3:1; 4:1; 7:32, 45, 47, 48; 8:13; 9:13, 15, 16, 40; 11:47–48, 57; 12:42; 18:3) and the chief priests (7:32, 45; 11:47, 57; 18:3, 35; 19:21; cf. 1:19) are mentioned as major opponents among the religious authorities, but there is no mention of Sadducees, elders, scribes, and Herodians.

8. Jesus dies giving "his life as a ransom for many" (10:45), but this concept, mentioned only once, is not developed.

Jesus' crucifixion is his moment of "glorification" (7:39; 11:4; 12:16, 23, 28; 13:31, 32; 14:13; 15:8; 17:4, 5; 21:19), identified (17:5) as the moment when his former glory was restored.

9. Jesus is portrayed (2:15–17) as having a special ministry to toll collectors, and "sinners," a societal grouping in Judaism whose members were not Torah observing.

There are no such groups in John (the man born blind and Jesus are called "sinners," but not because either belongs to a special social group; cf. 9:16, 24, 25).

10. Jesus refuses to give a public sign (8:11–13; but cf. 13:4 when he is addressed privately by his disciples).

The entire public career of Jesus is one of public "signs" (2:11, 23; 3:2; 4:48, 54; 6:2, 14, 26, 30; 7:31; 9:16; 10:41; 11:47; 12:18, 37; 20:30–31).

11. Peter is never "rehabilitated" after his denial of Jesus (14:66–72; cf. 16:7).

Peter is "rehabilitated" in John 21.

Differences in the Content of Events

Mark	John
1. Jesus is declared to be the Son of God by a heavenly voice at his baptism (1:11, although the narrator[6] had already shared this with the reader in 1:1).	Jesus was always the Son of God, i.e., he always existed with God (1:1).
2. Jesus is baptized by John in water (1:9–11).	John the Baptist does not baptize Jesus in water but only observes the "spirit descend as a dove from heaven" and remain upon Jesus (1:29–34).
3. The resurrection of Jesus is validated by the empty tomb (16:1–8).	The resurrection is validated by resurrection appearances (20:11–18, 19–23, 26–29; 21:1–17).[7]
4. During the last meal with his disciples, Jesus speaks the traditional words taken up into the Christian celebration of the "Lord's Supper": "This is my body"; "This is my blood" (14:22–25); only Luke gives the words "Do this in remembrance of me" (Luke 22:19), thus instituting the meal as a continuing celebration.	Jesus does not speak the traditional words instituting the "Lord's Supper." Rather Jesus washes the disciples' feet and directs them to follow his example by washing one another's feet (13:14).[8]
5. Jesus' last word from the cross is "My God, my God, why have you forsaken me?" (15:34).	Jesus' last word from the cross is "It is finished" (19:30).

∞ DIVERSITY AMONG MATTHEW, MARK, AND LUKE

Matthew, Mark, and Luke generally follow a common sequence of events. When one gospel diverges from the common order, the other two generally agree. Unlike Mark and John, the synoptic gospels generally use the same stories and sayings, use them in generally the same order, and narrate the same stories using regularly the same words. Yet striking differences among them remain. Differences exist in the narrative sequence of events and in the content of shared sayings. Yet their content and location in the narrative point clearly to them being the same saying.

One way of thinking about this problem is in terms of the kinds of material in the synoptics—how is the material similar and how it is different? Scholars identify basically seven classes of material.[9]

CLASS I: Material shared by Matthew, Mark, and Luke. Of approximately 480 verses shared by Matthew, Mark, and Luke, verbal agreement occurs with high frequency. Where wording in Matthew and Luke agrees, rarely does Mark disagree. And where Matthew and Luke follow the same sequence of events, Mark rarely disagrees.

CLASS II: Material shared by Matthew and Mark. Of the approximately 600 verses they have in common, 480 verses come from CLASS I, and there are 120 verses unique to Matthew and Mark. The shared material constitutes about 90% of Mark's gospel, but only 50% of Matthew.

CLASS III: Material shared by Mark and Luke. This amounts to approximately 24 verses plus the 480 verses of CLASS I. This shared material amounts to approximately half of Mark and one-third of Luke.

CLASS IV: Material shared by Matthew and Luke. About 170 shared verses are scattered throughout the two gospels. These consist primarily of John the Baptist traditions and Jesus' teaching material. These verses tend not to appear in the same sequence or context. Verbal similarities are not generally as high as CLASSES I–III, but sayings are almost verbatim in places.

CLASS V: Material unique to Mark. About 50 verses in Mark (around 10% of the gospel) do not appear in the other two gospels. This involves certain details in several stories that Mark shares with Matthew and Luke and two narratives unique to Mark: the healing of a deaf mute (7:32–37) and the healing of a blind man (8:22–26).

CLASS VI: Material unique to Matthew. About 280 verses appear in Matthew alone. They include birth narratives, resurrection appearances, and Jesus' teaching material having a Palestinian character with special Jewish interest.

CLASS VII: Material unique to Luke. About 500 verses appear only in Luke. They include birth narratives, infancy narratives, resurrection appearances, and numerous parables.

To illustrate the diversity/similarity among Matthew, Mark, and Luke several passages from CLASSES I, II, III, IV, VI/VII will be examined.

Two Different Birth and Infancy Narratives

Matthew 1:18–2:23

Luke 1:5–2:52

18Now the birth of Jesus Christ took place in this way. When his mother Mary had been betrothed to Joseph, before they came together she was found to be with child of the Holy Spirit; 19and her husband Joseph, being a just man and unwilling to put her to shame, resolved to divorce her quietly. 20But as he considered this, behold, an angel of the Lord appeared to him in a dream, saying, "Joseph, son of David, do not fear to take Mary your wife, for that which is conceived in her is of the Holy Spirit; 21she will bear a son, and you shall call his name Jesus, for he will save his people from their sins." 22All this took place to fulfil what the Lord had spoken by the prophet:
23"Behold, a virgin shall conceive and bear a son,
and his name shall be called Emmanuel" (which means, God with us). 24When Joseph woke from sleep, he did as the angel of the Lord commanded him; he took his wife, 25but knew her not until she had borne a son; and he called his name Jesus.
1Now when Jesus was born in Bethlehem of Judea in the days of Herod the king, behold, wise men from the East came to Jerusalem, saying, 2"Where is he who has been born king of the Jews? For we have seen his star in the East, and have come to worship him." 3When Herod the king heard this, he was troubled, and all Jerusalem with him; 4and assembling all the chief priests and scribes of the people, he inquired of them where the Christ was to be born. 5They told him, "In Bethlehem of Judea; for so it is written by the prophet:
6'And you, O Bethlehem, in the land of Judah, are by no means least among the rulers of Judah;
for from you shall come a ruler
who will govern my people Israel.' "
7Then Herod summoned the wise men secretly and ascertained from them what time the star appeared; 8and he sent

5In the days of Herod, king of Judea, there was a priest named Zechariah, of the division of Abijah; and he had a wife of the daughters of Aaron, and her name was Elizabeth. 6And they were both righteous before God, walking in all the commandments and ordinances of the Lord blameless. 7But they had no child, because Elizabeth was barren, and both were advanced in years.
8Now while he was serving as priest before God when his division was on duty, 9according to the custom of the priesthood, it fell to him by lot to enter the temple of the Lord and burn incense. 10And the whole multitude of the people were praying outside at the hour of incense. 11And there appeared to him an angel of the Lord standing on the right side of the altar of incense. 12And Zechariah was troubled when he saw him, and fear fell upon him. 13But the angel said to him, "Do not be afraid, Zechariah, for your prayer is heard, and your wife Elizabeth will bear you a son, and you shall call his name John. 14And you will have joy and gladness, and many will rejoice at his birth; 15for he will be great before the Lord, and he shall drink no wine nor strong drink, and he will be filled with the Holy Spirit, even from his mother's womb. 16And he will turn many of the sons of Israel to the Lord their God, 17and he will go before him in the spirit and power of Elijah, to turn the hearts of the fathers to the children, and the disobedient to the wisdom of the just, to make ready for the Lord a people prepared." 18And Zechariah said to the angel, "How shall I know this? For I am an old man, and my wife is advanced in years." 19And the angel answered him, "I am Gabriel, who stand in the presence of God; and I was sent to speak to you, and to bring you this good news. 20And behold, you will be silent and unable to speak until the day that these things come to pass, because you did not believe my words, which will be fulfilled in their time." 21And the people were waiting

them to Bethlehem, saying, "Go and search diligently for the child, and when you have found him bring me word, that I too may come and worship him." [9]When they had heard the king they went their way; and lo, the star which they had seen in the East went before them, till it came to rest over the place where the child was. [10]When they saw the star, they rejoiced exceedingly with great joy; [11]and going into the house they saw the child with Mary his mother, and they fell down and worshiped him. Then, opening their treasures, they offered him gifts, gold and frankincense and myrrh. [12]And being warned in a dream not to return to Herod, they departed to their own country by another way.

[13]Now when they had departed, behold, an angel of the Lord appeared to Joseph in a dream and said, "Rise, take the child and his mother, and flee to Egypt, and remain there till I tell you; for Herod is about to search for the child, to destroy him." [14]And he rose and took the child and his mother by night, and departed to Egypt, [15]and remained there until the death of Herod. This was to fulfil what the Lord had spoken by the prophet, "Out of Egypt have I called my son." [16]Then Herod, when he saw that he had been tricked by the wise men, was in a furious rage, and he sent and killed all the male children in Bethlehem and in all that region who were two years old or under, according to the time which he had ascertained from the wise men. [17]Then was fulfilled what was spoken by the prophet Jeremiah:

[18]"A voice was heard in Ramah,
wailing and loud lamentation,
Rachel weeping for her children;
she refused to be consoled, because
they were no more."

[19]But when Herod died, behold, an angel of the Lord appeared in a dream to Joseph in Egypt, saying, [20]"Rise, take the child and his mother, and go to the land of Israel, for those who sought the child's life are dead." [21]And he rose and took the child and his mother, and went to the land of Israel. [22]But when he heard that Archelaus reigned over Judea in place of his father Herod, he was afraid to go there, and

for Zechariah, and they wondered at his delay in the temple. [22]And when he came out, he could not speak to them, and they perceived that he had seen a vision in the temple; and he made signs to them and remained dumb. [23]And when his time of service was ended, he went to his home. [24]After these days his wife Elizabeth conceived, and for five months she hid herself, saying, [25]"Thus the Lord has done to me in the days when he looked on me, to take away my reproach among men."

[26]In the sixth month the angel Gabriel was sent from God to a city of Galilee named Nazareth, [27]to a virgin betrothed to a man whose name was Joseph, of the house of David; and the virgin's name was Mary. [28]And he came to her and said, "Hail, O favored one, the Lord is with you!" [29]But she was greatly troubled at the saying, and considered in her mind what sort of greeting this might be. [30]And the angel said to her, "Do not be afraid, Mary, for you have found favor with God. [31]And behold, you will conceive in your womb and bear a son, and you shall call his name Jesus. [32]He will be great, and will be called the Son of the Most High; and the Lord God will give to him the throne of his father David, [33]and he will reign over the house of Jacob for ever; and of his kingdom there will be no end." [34]And Mary said to the angel, "How shall this be, since I have no husband?" [35]And the angel said to her, "The Holy Spirit will come upon you, and the power of the Most High will overshadow you; therefore the child to be born will be called holy, the Son of God. [36]And behold, your kinswoman Elizabeth in her old age has also conceived a son; and this is the sixth month with her who was called barren. [37]For with God nothing will be impossible." [38]And Mary said, "Behold, I am the handmaid of the Lord; let it be to me according to your word." And the angel departed from her.

[39]In those days Mary arose and went with haste into the hill country, to a city of Judah, [40]and she entered the house of Zechariah and greeted Elizabeth. [41]And when Elizabeth heard the greeting of Mary, the babe leaped in her womb; and Elizabeth was filled with the Holy Spirit

being warned in a dream he withdrew to the district of Galilee. [23]And he went and dwelt in a city called Nazareth, that what was spoken by the prophets might be fulfilled, "He shall be called a Nazarene."

[42]and she exclaimed with a loud cry, "Blessed are you among women, and blessed is the fruit of your womb! [43]And why is this granted me, that the mother of my Lord should come to me? [44]For behold, when the voice of your greeting came to my ears, the babe in my womb leaped for joy. [45]And blessed is she who believed that there would be a fulfilment of what was spoken to her from the Lord." [46]And Mary said,

"My soul magnifies the Lord,
[47]and my spirit rejoices in God my
     Savior,
[48]for he has regarded the low estate
     of his handmaiden.
For behold, henceforth all
     generations will call me blessed;
[49]for he who is mighty has done great
     things for me,
and holy is his name.
[50]And his mercy is on those who fear
     him
from generation to generation.
[51]He has shown strength with his arm,
he has scattered the proud in the
     imagination of their hearts,
[52]he has put down the mighty from
     their thrones,
and exalted those of low degree;
[53]he has filled the hungry with good
     things,
and the rich he has sent empty away.
[54]He has helped his servant Israel,
in remembrance of his mercy,
[55]as he spoke to our fathers,
to Abraham and to his posterity for
     ever."

[56]And Mary remained with her about three months, and returned to her home.

[57]Now the time came for Elizabeth to be delivered, and she gave birth to a son. [58]And her neighbors and kinsfolk heard that the Lord had shown great mercy to her, and they rejoiced with her. [59]And on the eighth day they came to circumcise the child; and they would have named him Zechariah after his father, [60]but his mother said, "Not so; he shall be called John." [61]And they said to her, "None of your kindred is called by this name." [62]And they made signs to his father, inquiring what he would have him called. [63]And he asked for a writing tablet, and wrote, "His name is John." And they all

marveled. 64And immediately his mouth was opened and his tongue loosed, and he spoke, blessing God. 65And fear came on all their neighbors. And all these things were talked about through all the hill country of Judea; 66and all who heard them laid them up in their hearts, saying, "What then will this child be?" For the hand of the Lord was with him. 67And his father Zechariah was filled with the Holy Spirit, and prophesied, saying,

68"Blessed be the Lord God of Israel, for he has visited and redeemed his people,

69and has raised up a horn of salvation for us
    in the house of his servant David,

70as he spoke by the mouth of his holy prophets from of old,

71that we should be saved from our enemies, and from the hand of all who hate us;

72to perform the mercy promised to our fathers,
    and to remember his holy covenant,

73the oath which he swore to our father Abraham,

74to grant us that we, being delivered from the hand of our enemies,
    might serve him without fear, 75in holiness and righteousness
    before him all the days of our life.

76And you, child, will be called the prophet of the Most High;
    for you will go before the Lord to prepare his ways,

77to give knowledge of salvation to his people
    in the forgiveness of their sins,

78through the tender mercy of our God, when the day shall dawn upon us from on high

79to give light to those who sit in darkness and in the shadow of death,
to guide our feet into the way of peace."

80And the child grew and became strong in spirit, and he was in the wilderness till the day of his manifestation to Israel.

1In those days a decree went out from Caesar Augustus that all the world should be enrolled. 2This was the first enrollment, when Quirinius was governor of Syria. 3And all went to be enrolled, each to his own city. 4And Joseph

also went up from Galilee, from the city
of Nazareth, to Judea, to the city of
David, which is called Bethlehem, because he was of the house and lineage of
David, [5]to be enrolled with Mary, his betrothed, who was with child. [6]And while
they were there, the time came for her
to be delivered. [7]And she gave birth to
her first-born son and wrapped him in
swaddling cloths, and laid him in a manger, because there was no place for
them in the inn.

[8]And in that region there were shepherds out in the field, keeping watch
over their flock by night. [9]And an angel
of the Lord appeared to them, and the
glory of the Lord shone around them,
and they were filled with fear. [10]And the
angel said to them, "Be not afraid; for
behold, I bring you good news of a great
joy which will come to all the people;
[11]for to you is born this day in the city
of David a Savior, who is Christ the Lord.
[12]And this will be a sign for you: you will
find a babe wrapped in swaddling cloths
and lying in a manger." [13]And suddenly
there was with the angel a multitude of
the heavenly host praising God and saying, [14]"Glory to God in the highest, and
on earth peace among men with whom
he is pleased!"

[15]When the angels went away from them
into heaven, the shepherds said to one
another, "Let us go over to Bethlehem
and see this thing that has happened,
which the Lord has made known to us."
[16]And they went with haste, and found
Mary and Joseph, and the babe lying in a
manger. [17]And when they saw it they
made known the saying which had been
told them concerning this child; [18]and all
who heard it wondered at what the
shepherds told them. [19]But Mary kept all
these things, pondering them in her
heart. [20]And the shepherds returned,
glorifying and praising God for all they
had heard and seen, as it had been told
them.

[21]And at the end of eight days, when he
was circumcised, he was called Jesus,
the name given by the angel before he
was conceived in the womb.

[22]And when the time came for their purification according to the law of Moses,
they brought him up to Jerusalem to
present him to the Lord [23](as it is written

in the law of the Lord, "Every male that opens the womb shall be called holy to the Lord") 24and to offer a sacrifice according to what is said in the law of the Lord, "a pair of turtledoves, or two young pigeons." 25Now there was a man in Jerusalem, whose name was Simeon, and this man was righteous and devout, looking for the consolation of Israel, and the Holy Spirit was upon him. 26And it had been revealed to him by the Holy Spirit that he should not see death before he had seen the Lord's Christ. 27And inspired by the Spirit he came into the temple; and when the parents brought in the child Jesus, to do for him according to the custom of the law, 28he took him up in his arms and blessed God and said,

29"Lord, now lettest thou thy servant depart in peace, according to thy word;
30for mine eyes have seen thy salvation
31which thou hast prepared in the presence of all peoples,
32a light for revelation to the Gentiles, and for glory to thy people Israel."
33And his father and his mother marveled at what was said about him; 34and Simeon blessed them and said to Mary his mother, "Behold, this child is set for the fall and rising of many in Israel, and for a sign that is spoken against 35(and a sword will pierce through your own soul also), that thoughts out of many hearts may be revealed." 36And there was a prophetess, Anna, the daughter of Phanuel, of the tribe of Asher; she was of a great age, having lived with her husband seven years from her virginity, 37and as a widow till she was eighty-four. She did not depart from the temple, worshiping with fasting and prayer night and day. 38And coming up at that very hour she gave thanks to God, and spoke of him to all who were looking for the redemption of Jerusalem.
39And when they had performed everything according to the law of the Lord, they returned into Galilee, to their own city, Nazareth. 40And the child grew and became strong, filled with wisdom; and the favor of God was upon him.
41Now his parents went to Jerusalem every year at the feast of the Passover. 42And when he was twelve years old,

they went up according to custom; [43]and when the feast was ended, as they were returning, the boy Jesus stayed behind in Jerusalem. His parents did not know it, [44]but supposing him to be in the company they went a day's journey, and they sought him among their kinsfolk and acquaintances; [45]and when they did not find him, they returned to Jerusalem, seeking him. [46]After three days they found him in the temple, sitting among the teachers, listening to them and asking them questions; [47]and all who heard him were amazed at his understanding and his answers. [48]And when they saw him they were astonished; and his mother said to him, "Son, why have you treated us so? Behold, your father and I have been looking for you anxiously." [49]And he said to them, "How is it that you sought me? Did you not know that I must be in my Father's house?" [50]And they did not understand the saying which he spoke to them. [51]And he went down with them and came to Nazareth, and was obedient to them; and his mother kept all these things in her heart. [52]And Jesus increased in wisdom and in stature, and in favor with God and man.

These two different narratives are part of CLASSES VI and VII. Matthew has one cycle of narratives and Luke another. The differences are obvious. Matthew, on the one hand, tells the story of the "wise men from the East" (2:1–12), Jesus' family's flight to Egypt (2:13–15), Herod's massacre of the children (2:16–18), Jesus' family returns to Israel and settles in Nazareth (2:19–23). Luke, on the other hand, narrates the announcement of John the Baptist's birth (1:5–25), the announcement of Jesus' birth (1:26–38), Mary visits Elizabeth (1:39–56), the birth of John the Baptist (1:57–80), the birth of Jesus (2:1–7), angels appear to shepherds in a field (2:8–20), the circumcision and presentation of Jesus in the temple (2:21–40), and Jesus in the temple at twelve years of age (2:41–52).

Points of Agreement[10]

1. They both date the birth of Jesus in the reign of Herod the Great, (the king of Jewish Palestine who died in 4 B.C.E.): Matt 2:1/Luke

1:5; but compare Luke 2:2 where the birth of Jesus is associated with the census that Quirinius took in 6 C.E.

2. Jesus was born in Bethlehem but reared in Nazareth: Matt 2:5/Luke 2:4.

3. The mother of Jesus was Mary. She was a virgin at the time of Jesus' birth. The conception of Jesus is described as the creative act of the Holy Spirit: Matt 1:18–25/Luke 1:26–35.

4. Mary's husband was Joseph of the line of David; the two genealogies, although different, trace the lineage back through Joseph: Matt 1:15–16/Luke 3:23.

5. In both, Jesus is named in obedience to the command of an angel: Matt 1:21/Luke 1:31.

Points of Difference

Matthew	Luke
1. The announcement of Jesus' birth is made to Joseph in a dream (1:20–24).[11]	The announcement is made to Mary but not in a dream. (1:26–37).
2. Joseph plays a primary role in the story (1:18–25; 2:13–14, 19–23).	Joseph appears almost incidentally (named: 2:4, 16; alluded to: 2:5, 22, 27, 33, 39, 41, 48).
3. The story of the Magi (2:1–12).	Lacking in Luke.
4. Lacking in Matthew.	The story of the shepherds in the field (2:8–20).
5. The story of the massacre of the children (2:16–18); the house of Herod is featured in a prominent role in the story.	Lacking in Luke.
6. Jesus is apparently born in a house (2:11).	Jesus is born in a stable (2:7, 12, 16).
7. Bethlehem in Judea is the home of Mary and Joseph. They leave Bethlehem because of a warning in a dream and flee to Egypt. They do not return home to Bethlehem because they fear Herod's son Archaelaus, and hence go to Nazareth in Galilee (2:1, 18–23).	Nazareth in Galilee is the home of Mary and Joseph. They go to Bethlehem in Judea, because of the Roman census, to register in the city of Joseph's ancestor, David. After Jesus is born, they go to nearby Jerusalem to the temple (apparently not fearing Archaelaus) and then return home to Nazareth (1:26; 2:4–6, 22–24, 39–40).

8. Matthew explains the significance of the name Jesus and links it with Isaiah (1:21–23).

Lacking in Luke.

9. Lacking in Matthew.

Luke has a cycle of birth stories about John the Baptist (1:5–25, 57–80), and represents Jesus and John as kinsmen (1:36).

Variety among Resurrection Narratives

Matthew 28:1–8	Mark 16:1–8	Luke 24:1–11	John 20:1–13
[1]Now after the sabbath, toward the dawn of the first day of the week, Mary Magdalene and the other Mary went to see the sepulchre. [2]And behold, there was a great earthquake; for an angel of the Lord descended from heaven and came and rolled back the stone, and sat upon it. [3]His appearance was like lightning, and his raiment white as snow. [4]And for fear of him the guards trembled and became like dead men. [5]But the angel said to the women, "Do not be afraid; for I know that you seek Jesus who was crucified. [6]He is not here; for he has risen, as he said. Come, see the place where he lay. [7]Then go quickly and tell his disciples that he has risen from the dead, and behold, he is going before you to Galilee; there you will see him. Lo, I have told you." [8]So they departed quickly from the tomb with fear and great joy, and ran to tell his disciples.	[1]And when the sabbath was past, Mary Magdalene, and Mary the mother of James, and Salome, bought spices, so that they might go and anoint him. [2]And very early on the first day of the week they went to the tomb when the sun had risen. [3]And they were saying to one another, "Who will roll away the stone for us from the door of the tomb?" [4]And looking up, they saw that the stone was rolled back—it was very large. [5]And entering the tomb, they saw a young man sitting on the right side, dressed in a white robe; and they were amazed. [6]And he said to them, "Do not be amazed; you seek Jesus of Nazareth, who was crucified. He has risen, he is not here; see the place where they laid him. [7]But go, tell his disciples and Peter that he is going before you to Galilee; there you will see him, as he told you." [8]And they went out and fled from the tomb; for trembling and astonishment had come upon them; and they said nothing to any one, for they were afraid.	[1]But on the first day of the week, at early dawn, they went to the tomb, taking the spices which they had prepared. [2]And they found the stone rolled away from the tomb, [3]but when they went in they did not find the body. [4]While they were perplexed about this, behold, two men stood by them in dazzling apparel; [5]and as they were frightened and bowed their faces to the ground, the men said to them, "Why do you seek the living among the dead? [6]Remember how he told you, while he was still in Galilee, [7]that the Son of man must be delivered into the hands of sinful men, and be crucified, and on the third day rise." [8]And they remembered his words, [9]and returning from the tomb they told all this to the eleven and to all the rest. [10]Now it was Mary Magdalene and Joanna and Mary the mother of James and the other women with them who told this to the apostles; [11]but these words seemed to them an idle tale, and they did not believe them.	[1]Now on the first day of the week Mary Magdalene came to the tomb early, while it was still dark, and saw that the stone had been taken away from the tomb. [2]So she ran, and went to Simon Peter and the other disciple, the one whom Jesus loved, and said to them, "They have taken the Lord out of the tomb, and we do not know where they have laid him." [3]Peter then came out with the other disciple, and they went toward the tomb. [4]They both ran, but the other disciple outran Peter and reached the tomb first; [5]and stooping to look in, he saw the linen cloths lying there, but he did not go in. [6]Then Simon Peter came, following him, and went into the tomb; he saw the linen cloths lying, [7]and the napkin, which had been on his head, not lying with the linen cloths but rolled up in a place by itself. [8]Then the other disciple, who reached the tomb first, also went in, and he saw and believed; [9]for as yet they did not know the scripture, that he must rise from the dead. [10]Then the disciples went back to their homes. [11]But Mary stood weeping outside the tomb, and

as she wept she stooped to look into the tomb; [12]and she saw two angels in white, sitting where the body of Jesus had lain, one at the head and one at the feet. [13]They said to her, "Woman, why are you weeping?" She said to them, "Because they have taken away my Lord, and I do not know where they have laid him."

The segment that will be closely examined is CLASS I, but Matthew and Luke have other narratives in connection with the resurrection account that are CLASSES VI and VII. In other words, Matthew, Mark, and Luke are similar (yet quite different) in the segment that will be examined here. Matthew, Luke, and John have additional material that is not shared by each other or by Mark.

Mark: The earliest attested ending to Mark's gospel is 16:8. Mark records no resurrection appearances by Jesus.[12] The gospel ends with the women fleeing from the tomb in fear, saying nothing to anyone (16:8).

Matthew: Following the shared synoptic material portraying the women at the tomb, Matthew describes Jesus' appearing to the women as they were going to tell the disciples what they had seen (28:9–10), the bribing of the guards by the chief priests (28:11–15), and the great commission on a mountain in Galilee (28:16–20).

Luke: Following the shared material, Luke adds the appearance of Jesus to two disciples going to Emmaus (24:13–32), an appearance of Jesus to the eleven disciples (24:33–49), and Jesus blessing the disciples at Bethany (24:50–53).

John: John's narrative at the tomb of Jesus on Sunday morning departs dramatically from the synoptic accounts. John also adds unique material: an appearance of Jesus to Mary Magdalene alone at the tomb (20:11–18), an appearance to the disciples when Thomas was not present (20:19–25), an appearance to the disciples with Thomas present (20:26–30), and an appearance by Jesus to the disciples beside the sea (21:1–25).

In the material shared by Matthew, Mark, and Luke we find some striking differences.

	Matthew	Mark	Luke	John
1. Who went to the tomb?	Mary Magdalene and the other Mary (28:1)	Mary Magdalene and Mary the mother of James, and Salome (16:1)	Mary Magdalene, Joanna, and Mary the mother of James and the other women with them (24:10)	Mary Magdalene, and later Simon Peter and the disciple whom Jesus loved (20:1–3)
2. Why did they go?	To see the sepulchre (28:1)	To anoint the body of Jesus (16:1)	To anoint the body of Jesus (24:1; cf. 23:56)	No reason is given
3. What was the condition of the tomb?	While the women watched, an angel rolled back the stone from the opening of the tomb (28:2)	The stone sealing the opening of the tomb was already rolled back (16:4)	The stone sealing the opening of the tomb was already rolled back (24:2)	The stone sealing the opening of the tomb was already rolled back (20:1)
4. Whom did they find at the tomb?	Only the guards were there initially, and then an angel appeared outside the tomb. The women apparently do not enter the tomb (28:2–8)	A young man was inside the tomb, sitting on the right side, when the women entered (16:5)	No one is there initially, but then suddenly two men in dazzling apparel stood by the women after they entered the tomb (24:4)	Mary Magdalene found no one there initially and she did not enter the tomb. Later Simon Peter and the disciple whom Jesus loved entered the tomb. When they departed, Mary stoops down to peer inside and sees two angels in white sitting where the body of Jesus had been lying (20:1–12)
5. How was/were the person(s) at the tomb dressed?	His clothing was as white as snow (28:3)	He was dressed in a white robe (16:5)	They wore dazzling apparel (24:4)	They were dressed in white (20:11)
6. Where were the disciples told to go?	They were told to go to Galilee (28:7)	They were told to go to Galilee (16:7)	They were told to stay in Jerusalem (24:49)	They were given no directions to go anywhere.

Variety in the Accounts of the Baptism of Jesus

Matthew 3:13–17	Mark 1:9–11	Luke 3:21–22	John 1:29–34
[13]Then Jesus came from Galilee to the Jordan to John, to be baptized by him. [14]John would have prevented him, saying, "I need to be baptized by you, and do you come to me?" [15]But Jesus answered him, "Let it be so now; for thus it is fitting for us to fulfil all righteousness." Then he consented. [16]And when Jesus was baptized, he went up immediately from the water, and behold, the heavens were opened and he saw the Spirit of God descending like a dove, and alighting on him; [17]and lo, a voice from heaven, saying, "This is my beloved Son, with whom I am well pleased."	[9]In those days Jesus came from Nazareth of Galilee and was baptized by John in the Jordan. [10]And when he came up out of the water, immediately he saw the heavens opened and the Spirit descending upon him like a dove; [11]and a voice came from heaven, "Thou art my beloved Son; with thee I am well pleased."	[21]Now when all the people were baptized, and when Jesus also had been baptized and was praying, the heaven was opened, [22]and the Holy Spirit descended upon him in bodily form, as a dove, and a voice came from heaven, "Thou art my beloved Son; with thee I am well pleased."	[29]The next day he saw Jesus coming toward him, and said, "Behold, the Lamb of God, who takes away the sin of the world! [30]This is he of whom I said, 'After me comes a man who ranks before me, for he was before me.' [31]I myself did not know him; but for this I came baptizing with water, that he might be revealed to Israel." [32]And John bore witness, "I saw the Spirit descend as a dove from heaven, and it remained on him. [33]I myself did not know him; but he who sent me to baptize with water said to me, 'He on whom you see the Spirit descend and remain, this is he who baptizes with the Holy Spirit.' [34]And I have seen and have borne witness that this is the Son of God."

Matthew, Mark, and Luke describe Jesus' baptism in similar, yet different ways. The Gospel of John does not describe a water baptism of Jesus and hence cannot be compared in this regard.

Matthew and Mark report unequivocally that John baptized Jesus (Matt 3:13–14; Mark 1:9). Luke's gospel, however, does not say who baptized Jesus, but in Luke's sequence of events it occurred *after* John had been put in prison by Herod (Luke 3:20–21). Mark and Luke never give a reason for Jesus' baptism, but Matthew explains it was done "to fulfill all righteousness" (Matt 3:13–15). Thus in Matthew Jesus' baptism was clearly not a "baptism of repentance for the forgiveness of sins" (Mark 1:4–5), as one might conclude from Mark 1:9. In Luke, on the other hand, Jesus' baptism is not associated with John's "baptism of repentance." Thus both Matthew and Luke can be seen as "correctives" of Mark.

All three gospels describe the descent of the spirit differently. In Mark, the spirit descends on Jesus "like a dove" (Mark 1:10). The Greek participle may simply describe how the spirit descended, i.e., as gracefully as a dove descends. In short, the spirit is not unambiguously personified in Mark. Matthew more clearly describes the personification of the spirit as a dove: the spirit descends and "alights" on Jesus (Matt 3:16). Luke describes a dove, in which the spirit is embodied, descending upon Jesus (Luke 3:22).

Matthew and Mark describe the baptism of Jesus and the descent of the spirit as two stages of one event. Jesus was immersed in water and immediately as he came up from the water the spirit descended on him (Matt 3:16; Mark 1:10). In Luke, however, the water baptism itself is not described in any detail. Luke says that after Jesus and all the people were baptized, the spirit (later?) descended on Jesus while he was praying (Luke 3:21–22). In other words, in Luke the water baptism and the spirit baptism constitute two separate events, whereas in Matthew and Mark they are sequential parts of the same event.

Finally, the voice from heaven addresses two different audiences. In Matthew the voice apparently speaks to others present at the event: "This is my beloved son" (Matt 3:17). In Mark and Luke the voice addresses Jesus only: "You are my beloved son" (Mark 1:11; Luke 3:22).

The report of Jesus' baptism in the Gospel of John differs remarkably. Jesus is not described as he is being baptized in water at the hands of John. Rather, the descent of the spirit on Jesus, which John the baptizer claims to have seen (John 1:32–34), takes center stage. John's public activity of baptizing in some way had the goal of "revealing Jesus to Israel," but it is not clear how that was accomplished in respect to Jesus (John 1:31).

Close Similarity and Diversity in the Temptation Narratives

Matthew 4:1–11	Mark 1:12–13	Luke 4:1–13
[1]Then Jesus was led up by the Spirit into the wilderness to be tempted by the devil. [2]And he fasted forty days and forty nights, and afterward he was hungry.	[12]The Spirit immediately drove him out into the wilderness. [13]And he was in the wilderness forty days, tempted by Satan; and he was with the wild beasts; and the angels ministered to him.	[1]And Jesus, full of the Holy Spirit, returned from the Jordan, and was led by the Spirit [2]for forty days in the wilderness, tempted by the devil. And he ate nothing in those days; and when they were ended, he was hungry.

[3]And the tempter came and said to him, "If you are the Son of God, command these stones to become loaves of bread." [4]But he answered, "It is written, 'Man shall not live by bread alone, but by every word that proceeds from the mouth of God.'" [5]Then the devil took him to the holy city, and set him on the pinnacle of the temple, [6]and said to him, "If you are the Son of God, throw yourself down; for it is written, 'He will give his angels charge of you,' and 'On their hands they will bear you up, lest you strike your foot against a stone.'" [7]Jesus said to him, "Again it is written, 'You shall not tempt the Lord your God.'" [8]Again, the devil took him to a very high mountain, and showed him all the kingdoms of the world and the glory of them; [9]and he said to him, "All these I will give you, if you will fall down and worship me." [10]Then Jesus said to him, "Begone, Satan! for it is written, 'You shall worship the Lord your God and him only shall you serve.'" [11]Then the devil left him, and behold, angels came and ministered to him.

[3]The devil said to him, "If you are the Son of God, command this stone to become bread." [4]And Jesus answered him, "It is written, 'Man shall not live by bread alone.'" [5]And the devil took him up, and showed him all the kingdoms of the world in a moment of time, [6]and said to him, "To you I will give all this authority and their glory; for it has been delivered to me, and I give it to whom I will. [7]If you, then, will worship me, it shall all be yours." [8]And Jesus answered him, "It is written, 'You shall worship the Lord your God, and him only shall you serve.'" [9]And he took him to Jerusalem, and set him on the pinnacle of the temple, and said to him, "If you are the Son of God, throw yourself down from here; [10]for it is written, 'He will give his angels charge of you, to guard you,' [11]and 'On their hands they will bear you up, lest you strike your foot against a stone.'" [12]And Jesus answered him, "It is said, 'You shall not tempt the Lord your God.'" [13]And when the devil had ended every temptation, he departed from him until an opportune time.

Mark's schematic treatment of the temptation of Jesus is surprising in light of the close similarity between Matthew and Luke. Matthew and Luke narrate a dialogue between Jesus and his tempter. Mark's brief note alludes to a temptation, but does not describe it. Reading closely, a reader will see a progressive "improvement" from Mark to Matthew to Luke in their descriptions of Jesus. In Mark the spirit drives Jesus into the wilderness, but in Matthew the spirit "leads" Jesus. Luke presents a much more pietistic picture of Jesus: Jesus, "full of the Holy Spirit," is "led by the spirit" into the wilderness. In the light of Matthew and Luke, Mark's Jesus appears driven against his will into the wilderness, the haunt of the evil spirits. A great distance emerges between the images created by the narratives of Mark and Luke.

Mark's "wild beasts" do not appear in Matthew and Luke. The length of time that Jesus stays in the wilderness is also slightly different. Mark and Luke agree the time frame was forty days. But

Matthew has Jesus in the wilderness forty days and forty nights, a slightly longer period of time if the expression is strictly literal—since it is possible to stay forty days and not forty nights. The narratives also give different names for the tempter. In Mark, Satan tempts Jesus. In Luke, the tempter is the devil. Matthew, for the most part, agrees with Luke that the devil tempts Jesus, but in Matt 4:10 Jesus uses "Satan" when addressing the tempter.

Matthew and Luke report three temptations: the challenge to turn stones to bread; the taunt for Jesus to throw himself down from the "pinnacle" of the temple; and the devil's offer of the kingdoms of the world in exchange for worship. But their order varies in each gospel. In Matthew the order is bread-pinnacle-kingdoms, while in Luke the order appears as bread-kingdoms-pinnacle. Similar language recurs in each temptation, but with interesting variations:

Matthew	Luke
these stones to become loaves of bread (4:3)	this stone to become bread (4:3)
but by every word proceeding from God's mouth (4:4)	lacking in Luke
holy city (4:5)	Jerusalem (4:9)
lacking in Matthew	"from here" and "to guard you" (4:10)
Matthew reads "again" (4:7,8)	lacking in Luke
"to a very high mountain" and "the glory of them" (4:8)	lacking in Luke
lacking in Matthew	"in a moment of time" (4:5)
lacking in Matthew	"authority and glory given to me, and I give it to whom I will" (4:6)
"Begone, Satan" (4:10)	lacking in Luke

In their concluding lines the narratives of all three gospels are quite different. Luke says the devil ended "every temptation," thus suggesting that the three given in the temptation scene are merely examples of the kinds of temptations Jesus experienced. No such suggestion appears in Matthew. In Matthew the devil leaves Jesus alone, but in Luke he leaves him alone temporarily, until there was a more opportune time to tempt him. Matthew and Mark have angels coming to "minister" to Jesus.

Each gospel concludes with Jesus in a different location. In Luke, Jesus had been carried by the devil to the temple in Jerusalem (Luke 4:9) from his original position in the desert (Luke 4:1–2).

Matthew, however, begins and ends with Jesus outside of the city (Matt 4:1–2, 8). He only visits the "holy city" during the course of his temptations (Matt 4:5).

Subtle Differences in the Healing of Peter's Mother-in-Law

Matthew 8:14–15	Mark 1:29–31	Luke 4:38–39
[14]And when Jesus entered Peter's house, he saw his mother-in-law lying sick with a fever; [15]he touched her hand, and the fever left her, and she rose and served him.	[29]And immediately he left the synagogue, and entered the house of Simon and Andrew, with James and John. [30]Now Simon's mother-in-law lay sick with a fever, and immediately they told him of her. [31]And he came and took her by the hand and lifted her up, and the fever left her; and she served them.	[38]And he arose and left the synagogue, and entered Simon's house. Now Simon's mother-in-law was ill with a high fever, and they besought him for her. [39]And he stood over her and rebuked the fever, and it left her; and immediately she rose and served them.

This very brief miracle story reflects the typical form of such stories in antiquity: (1) the problem, (2) the miraculous deed, (3) a demonstration of the healing. But all three narratives, in spite of their obvious similarities, have subtle differences influencing how readers conceive the story. Each gospel creates a remarkably different image for the reader.

In Matthew, Jesus enters Peter's house alone where he sees Peter's (?) mother-in-law sick with a fever. In Mark, Jesus, along with James and John, enter a house described as belonging to both Simon and Andrew. Apparently James and John had to tell him Simon's mother-in-law was sick with a fever. In other words, Jesus himself does not immediately perceive her condition. In Luke, Jesus alone enters Simon's house when "they" (it is unclear who "they" are) "implore" him on behalf of Simon's mother-in-law, who was ill with a "high" fever. Luke intensifies the situation by making her illness more severe (i.e., "high fever"), and hence the earnest request (i.e., "implore") for her healing by others who were present.

In Matthew, Jesus touched her hand, and (in that instant) the fever left her. Then she rose and served *him*. In Mark, he took her by the hand, lifted her up, and then the fever left her. Then she served *them*. In Luke, Jesus stood over her and, using only words, commanded the fever to leave her. It was not (apparently) necessary for Jesus to touch her in order to effect the healing. Immediately she served *them*.

Sayings That Are Virtually Verbatim

John's Preaching of Repentance

Matthew 3:7–10	Luke 3:7–9
[7]But when he saw many of the Pharisees and Sadducees coming for baptism, he said to them, "You brood of vipers! Who warned you to flee from the wrath to come? [8]Bear fruit that befits repentance, [9]and do not presume to say to yourselves, 'We have Abraham as our father'; for I tell you, God is able from these stones to raise up children to Abraham. [10]Even now the axe is laid to the root of the trees; every tree therefore that does not bear good fruit is cut down and thrown into the fire."	[7]He said therefore to the multitudes that came out to be baptized by him, "You brood of vipers! Who warned you to flee from the wrath to come? [8]Bear fruits that befit repentance, and do not begin to say to yourselves, 'We have Abraham as our father'; for I tell you, God is able from these stones to raise up children to Abraham. [9]Even now the axe is laid to the root of the trees; every tree therefore that does not bear good fruit is cut down and thrown into the fire."

This brief pericope is virtually verbatim in each gospel. Only three differences exist between Matthew and Luke's performance of this saying by John the Baptist. A unique literary frame introduces each. In Matthew, John addresses his opponents: the Pharisees and the Sadducees. In Luke, however, John addresses the multitudes coming to him for baptism. The setting and saying make a rather odd combination in Luke. People coming for baptism had obviously already been warned and were in the process of repenting, which makes John's statement in Luke appear ungracious and inappropriate.

The saying itself is the same in both gospels except for the following: Matt 3:8 reads "fruit that befits of repentance" and Luke 3:8 reads "fruits that befit of repentance"; Matt 3:8 reads "presume to say" and Luke 3:8 reads "begin to say." A third difference is not recognizable in the English translation. In the phrase concerning the ax's being laid to the trees, Luke includes an intensive particle that Matthew does not have.[13]

Serving Two Masters

Matthew 6:24	Luke 16:13
[24] No *one* can serve two masters; for a slave will either hate the one and love the other, or be devoted to the one and despise the other. You cannot serve God and wealth. (NRSV)	[13] No *slave* can serve two masters; for a slave will either hate the one and love the other, or be devoted to the one and despise the other. You cannot serve God and wealth. (NRSV)

With one slight exception, this brief saying is identical in Matthew and Luke. Mark does not report it. Matthew reads "No *one* can serve two masters" while Luke reads "No *slave* can serve two masters."

Matthew 11:25–27	Luke 10:21–22
25 (At that time Jesus said,) "I thank you, Father, Lord of heaven and earth, because you have *hidden* these things from the wise and the intelligent and have revealed them to infants; 26 yes, Father, for such was your gracious will. 27 All things have been handed over to me by my Father, and *no one knows the Son* except the Father, *and no one knows the Father* except the Son and anyone to whom the Son chooses to reveal him." (NRSV)	21 (At that same hour Jesus rejoiced in the Holy Spirit and said,) "I thank you, Father, Lord of heaven and earth, because you have *hidden* these things from the wise and the intelligent and have revealed them to infants; 26 yes, Father, for such was your gracious will. 27 All things have been handed over to me by my Father, and *no one knows who the Son is* except the Father, *or who the Father is* except the Son and anyone to whom the Son chooses to reveal him." (NRSV)

Matthew and Luke use different Greek synonyms where the English translates *hidden*. Matthew reads ἔκρυψας and Luke reads ἀπέκρυψας. Another, more significant difference occurs later: Matthew says, *no one knows the Son* [οὐδεὶς ἐπιγινώσκει τὸν υἱόν], whereas Luke says, *no one knows who the Son is* [οὐδεὶς γινώσκει τίς ἐστιν ὁ υἱός]. Matthew reads, *and no one knows the Father* [οὐδὲ τὸν πατέρα τις ἐπιγινώσκει], whereas Luke reports, *or who the Father is* [καὶ τίς ἐστιν ὁ πατήρ]. Apart from these two exceptions the accounts are identical.

Woes on Galilean Cities (Matt 11:21–24, Luke 10:12–15)

Matthew 11:21–24	Luke 10:12–15
21"Woe to you, Chorazin! woe to you, Bethsaida! for if the mighty works done in you had been done in Tyre and Sidon, they would have repented long ago in sackcloth and ashes. 22But I tell you, it shall be more tolerable on the day of judgment for Tyre and Sidon than for you. 23And you, Capernaum, will you be exalted to heaven? You shall be brought down to Hades. For if the mighty works done in you had been done in Sodom, it would have remained until this day. 24But I tell you that it shall be more tolerable on the day of judgment for the land of Sodom than for you."	12"I tell you, it shall be more tolerable on that day for Sodom than for that town. 13"Woe to you, Chorazin! woe to you, Bethsaida! for if the mighty works done in you had been done in Tyre and Sidon, they would have repented long ago, sitting in sackcloth and ashes. 14But it shall be more tolerable in the judgment for Tyre and Sidon than for you. 15And you, Capernaum, will you be exalted to heaven? You shall be brought down to Hades."

This brief saying appears in two different literary contexts in Matthew and Luke. In Matthew it is included in Jesus' speech (Matt 11:7–30) to the crowds about John the Baptist (Matt 11:7). In Luke it falls into Jesus' speech commissioning the seventy (Luke 10:1–16). The few inconsistencies between the two performances of the saying are insignificant. Matthew and Luke each use a different form of the same Greek verb translated "had been done": Matthew (11:21) uses an aorist middle and Luke (10:13) uses an aorist passive. Luke (10:13) reads "sitting" before "in sackcloth and ashes," thus making the image more graphic. Matthew (11:22) reads the more emphatic, but unnecessary, "I tell you," which Luke does not have. Where Luke reads "in the judgment" (10:14), Matthew reads more dramatically "on the day of judgment" (11:22). Luke uses an unnecessary Greek article with "Hades" in 10:15, which Matthew does not have. Luke (10:12) leads the series of woes with a saying on Sodom, while Matthew (11:24) follows the series of woes with a saying on Sodom. Aside from these few differences the sayings are the same.

A saying on asking and receiving (Matt 7:7–8; Luke 11:9–10) and the parable of the Leaven (Matt 13:33; Luke 13:21) are verbatim.

∞

These examples illustrate the rather diverse ways the early Christian gospels narrate their stories of Jesus. The evidence ranges from verbatim accounts to widely differing descriptions of the same incident. The differences and similarities raise two fundamental questions for the historian desiring to reconstruct aspects of the public career of Jesus. (1) How can this surprising blend of similarity and difference among the early Christian gospels be plausibly explained? "Plausibly" means to provide a credible explanation to persons who have no agenda to protect a particular view of the gospels. Those who intuitively "know" the character of these texts without first examining them are unlikely to find any explanation other than their own prior explanation "plausible." For others, a plausible explanation begins by first considering the evidence and then proposing a reasonable solution that best accounts for the evidence. Of course, what is reasonable to one may not be reasonable to another, and that is why one proceeds toward a credible solution on the basis of the analysis and evaluation of evidence. (2) How does one know which traditions go back to the historical man? This question arises naturally where there are conflicting traditions. For example, did John the Baptist baptize Jesus as Matthew and Mark unequivocally state, or did he not baptize Jesus as the Gospel of John clearly says and as can be inferred from Luke? The first of these two fundamental questions will be addressed in the next chapter, and the second will be taken up subsequently.

∞ RECOMMENDED READING AND SOURCES CONSULTED

ALAND, KURT, ed. *Synopsis of the Four Gospels*. New York: United Bible Societies, 1982. BEARE, F. W. *The Earliest Records of Jesus*. Nashville: Abingdon, 1962. CROSSAN, J. D. *Sayings Parallels: A Workbook for the Jesus Tradition*. Philadelphia: Fortress, 1986. FARMER, W. R. *Synopticon: The Verbal Agreement between the Texts of Matthew, Mark, and Luke Contextually Exhibited*. Cambridge: Cambridge University Press, 1969. KLOPPENBORG, MEYER, et al. *Q-Thomas Reader*. ORCHARD, J. B. *A Synopsis of the Four Gospels in a New Translation Arranged According to the Two Document Hypothesis*. Mercer: University Press, 1982. SANDERS and DAVIES. *Studying the Synoptic Gospels*. Pages 51–61. THROCKMORTON, B. H. *Gospel Parallels: A Synopsis of the First Three Gospels with Alternative Readings from the Manuscripts and Noncanonical Parallels*. 5th rev. ed. New York: Thomas Nelson, 1992.

∞ ISSUES FOR STUDY AND DISCUSSION

In order to appreciate the nature of the problem, the student needs to compare the gospel texts. It is always preferable to use the Greek and Coptic texts, but the analysis can be done effectively with an English translation as well.

1. *Compare the following segments carefully noting all similarities and differences:*
   a. The image of the fig tree, Matt 24:32–36, Mark 13:28–32, Luke 21:29–33.
   b. Jesus' lament over Jerusalem, Matt 23:37–39, Luke 13:34–35.
   c. The story of the return of the evil spirit, Matt 12:43–45, Luke 11:24–26.
   d. Sayings on following Jesus, Matt 8:18–22, Luke 9:57–62.

2. *Compare the genealogies in Matt 1:2–17 and Luke 3:23–38. What are the points of similarity and how are they different? Identify parallels to this material in the Hebrew Bible. What conclusions do you draw from your analysis?*

3. *Closely compare the beatitudes in Matt 5:3–12 and Luke 6:20b–23. How are they similar and different? How many beatitudes are there? What do you conclude from your analysis?*

4. *Why does Jesus speak in parables? Compare Matt 13:10–17, Mark 4:10–12, Luke 8:9–10. In what ways do the gospels agree/disagree as to why Jesus used parables? Why do you think Jesus used parables? Why do you suppose there are no parables in the Gospel of John?*

5. *Compare Matt 18:10–14 (in the context of Matt 18:1–19:1), Luke 15:1–7, and the* Gospel of Thomas *logion 107. How are the two passages in Matthew and Luke similar and different? Are the parables in each gospel the same parable or are they different? To whom did Jesus tell this/these parable(s)? What do the evangelists give as the meaning(s) of the parable(s)?*

6. *Compare Matt 13:44–46 with the* Gospel of Thomas *logia 76 and 109. How are the parables similar and different? Are they all the same parable, different parables, or different performances of the same parable that simply differ with each performance? What do you conclude from this analysis?*

7. *Compare the similarities and differences among Matt 17:14–21, Mark 9:14–29, Luke 9:37–43a. Are they the same stories? Which of the three gospels are the most alike? If they are the same story, how do you explain Mark's being longer than Matthew's and Luke's? Has Mark elaborated, or have Matthew and Luke abbreviated?*

8. *Compare Matt 12:38–42, Mark 8:11–12, Luke 11:29–32. Are these accounts describing the same incident? If they are, how do you explain the fact that in Mark Jesus gives no sign to the Pharisees, while in Matthew and Luke he gives them the "sign of Jonah"? How do you explain the fact that Luke's Jesus gives a single explanation for the "sign of Jonah," while in Matthew there are two?*

9. *Compare the parable of the Mustard Seed in Matt 13:31–32, Mark 4:30–32, Luke 13:18–19 and list any differences. Are these differences significant? Do they create a different image in your mind? How do you explain the differences? What conclusions do you draw from your analysis?*

10. *Note the various accounts of the Last Supper: Matt 26:26–29, Mark 14:22–25, Luke 22:15–20. Why do you suppose Luke apparently reports two cups, but Matthew and Mark describe only one? Do they all agree that the "supper" was something the disciples should continue to perform in Jesus' memory? What is the most plausible explanation for this mix of similarity and diversity? What conclusions do you draw from your analysis?*

5

EXPLAINING THE DIVERSITY AND SIMILARITY IN THE GOSPELS

The recognition that the canonical gospels differ among themselves is not new. The differences were already recognized by the ancient church and pointed out by its opponents by the end of the second century—almost as soon as the four gospels began to be used together. The variations among the gospels in substance and in sequence of material raised questions as to their reliability for Christians of the late second century. The early Christian theologian Origen (185–234 C.E.), for example, addressing the issue of diversity, argued that there was only one "gospel," although it was presented in the form of four "gospels." In this way Origen argued for the "philosophical" unity of the gospel message preached by the church in the face of the formal disunity among the gospels themselves.

Several harmonies of the gospels were written during this early period. The best known of these was by Tatian (middle second century).[1] By eliminating and combining material, Tatian consolidated Matthew, Mark, Luke, and

John into a single narrative, called the *Diatessaron;* it was literally one gospel *through (dia)* the *four (tessarōn)* gospels.

Augustine (354–430) was the first to develop a theory for explaining the relationship among the gospels; his study was intended to clear up their discrepancies. But the complexity of the problem was not fully appreciated until the latter half of the eighteenth century when critical study of the New Testament emerged. Since that time, numerous theories have been advanced to explain the phenomenon of diversity/similarity among the gospels. This chapter will consider and evaluate some popular solutions used today.

∞ APPROACHES TOWARD A SOLUTION

The diversity, disunity, lack of harmony, and contradictions among the gospels suggest to some that the gospels are unreliable and thus cannot be trusted as historical accounts. If the gospels are unreliable historical records, so it is reasoned, how can they be trusted to communicate divine and eternal truth? Such logic demands a resolution of the diversity among the gospels.

Each of the three popular approaches to resolving the problems assumes that the gospels reflect precise descriptions of historical events in Palestine during the public career of Jesus. I label these proposed solutions *theological, historical,* and *harmonizing* explanations. For the most part, they seek to resolve the difficulties created when history and faith collide.

The Theological Explanation

The theological explanation acknowledges the diversity among the gospels but argues that this mixture of similarity and diversity is precisely what God wanted for reasons that we humans do not understand. The diversity and similarity among the gospels are construed as part of God's plan. Human beings, so the argument goes, are not expected to understand it. A basic premise of this explanation is that the very existence and precise form of the texts are God's doing.

In keeping with this premise, the verbatim or nearly verbatim passages in the gospels are regarded as having been made that way for emphasis, so as to eliminate any misunderstanding. That is why the gospels narrate their stories in the same way—so the reasoning goes. The issue of the gospels' diversity, however, remains a serious problem to be resolved. What kind of divine plan would have allowed so much confusion among texts held in such high regard by the church? Often the response is simply a reaffirmation of the original premise: "We are not supposed to understand!" Despite its good intentions, however, this explanation eventually undermines confidence in the texts.

A variation on this explanation eliminates the gospels' diversity by appealing to the integrity of the *autographs*. It is argued that the Jewish Scriptures (i.e., Old Testament) and the New Testament, as originally composed by their authors, were unified and harmonious. They had none of the diversity, disunity, lack of harmony, and contradictions that characterize the current texts of the gospels.[2] Thus, only the autographs were "without error." Diversity has crept into the texts during their transmission through the centuries. Since the autographs do not exist, however, this theory cannot be tested. In any case this explanation fails to take seriously the diversity and similarity among the gospels that we do possess.

The Historical Explanation

The historical explanation assumes that the writers of the gospels were eyewitnesses. But there are episodes in which no one but Jesus was present; consequently, the existence of the report itself cannot be explained on the basis of "eyewitness testimony." For example, who overheard the exchange between Jesus and the devil reported in the temptation narrative(s)? No one other than Jesus was present to observe the details and overhear the nearly verbatim agreement in the dialogue between Jesus and the devil in Luke 4:1–13 and Matt 4:1–11. Furthermore, who overheard Jesus' prayer at Gethsemane (Mark 14:32–42=Matt 26:36–46=Luke 22:39–46)? Although an early tradition that Jesus prayed prior to his crucifixion exists (Heb 5:7), the specific wording of that prayer does not stem from eyewitness testimony, since there were no eyewitnesses.

Assuming the gospel writers were eyewitnesses, diversity is to be expected, since not everyone hears, sees, or experiences events in the same way. In courtroom deliberations, for example, attorneys expect some difference in eyewitness testimony simply because of the way events are perceived. Each attorney develops a strategy for the case based on the similar and diverging testimony of the eyewitnesses, and then tries to convince the jury that their witnesses' perception of the event is the closest to reality. Testimonies vary because perspectives and perceptions of witnesses differ. A telling example of diverging testimony appears in the eyewitness accounts of the assassination of President John F. Kennedy in 1963. Although everyone agreed that the president was assassinated, eyewitness testimony differs on the number of assassins and even on the number of shots fired.[3]

If the gospel writers were eyewitnesses, such a theory of eyewitness reporting could account for much of their diversity. Yet such a theory fails to explain adequately the verbatim and nearly verbatim material. If we expect diversity from eyewitnesses, what are we to say about the verbatim or virtually identical material? In a modern courtroom setting, if the witnesses testify using exactly the same words, the inference could easily be that witnesses were coached and had memorized their testimony. Verbatim reports are not likely to occur, however, without the use of written texts, where the narrative is stabilized to allow exact memorization. In an oral and uncontrolled environment one might expect similar reports, but verbatim or nearly verbatim reports under such conditions is surprising. Hence under the "historical explanation" the verbatim and virtually identical passages become an insurmountable problem to the assumption that the gospels are eyewitnesses accounts.[4]

The Harmonizing Explanation

The harmonizing explanation takes various forms but each assumes that the canonical evangelists report historical events substantially as they occurred. Hence, the reported events in the gospels accurately represent historical events in first-century Palestine. In order to reconstruct the historical event behind the gospels one simply looks for an explanation that accommodates what each evangelist reports.[5] That is to say, one looks for a common denominator to the parallel reports that allows each report to be essentially correct. In effect, the parallel reports are harmonized.

For example, the discrepancy as to when Jesus cleansed the temple (Matthew/Mark/Luke—at the beginning of his public career; John—at the end) has been resolved by assuming that Jesus cleansed the temple on two separate occasions.[6] This solution allows both the synoptic gospels and John's gospel to be at least partially correct, but it does not account for the fact that early Christian texts uniformly report only one cleansing of the temple. Even the *Diatessaron* reports only one cleansing (*Diatessaron* 32). Proposing that there were two cleansings of the temple is a modern invention intended to resolve this ancient discrepancy between John and the synoptic gospels.

The discrepancy between the two different genealogies for Jesus reported in Matthew and Luke is a second example. To resolve this rather glaring lack of uniformity and maintain the agreement of the gospels, some have argued that Luke is reporting Mary's genealogy rather than Joseph's[7]—in spite of the fact that Luke unambiguously traces the descent of Jesus through Joseph: Jesus was the supposed son of Joseph, who was the son of Heli (Luke 3:23). The genealogy that follows, at least according to Luke, is Joseph's; Mary is not mentioned. The argument upholds Luke's harmony with Matthew at the cost of Luke's integrity and clarity. Such an argument must assume that Luke is deliberately obscure or at best simply careless.

Such a resolution overlooks the fact that before the gospels were collected by the church into their present fourfold canonical configuration (by the end of the second century), each would have initially been used independently in the ancient world. An entire generation of early Christians probably knew only one gospel. For Christians who knew only the Gospel of Luke there was only one cleansing of the temple, and Luke's genealogy would hardly have been thought to be Mary's genealogy.

The harmonizing explanation ultimately compromises and undermines the reliability of all the evangelists. It assumes that none of the evangelists knew the full story, and that they are all, at least partially, incorrect because the full account can be known only by reading all of the gospels together. Furthermore, some of the discrepancies cannot comfortably be harmonized. For example, was the last supper that Jesus celebrated with his disciples a Passover meal, as Matthew, Mark, and Luke report, or did it take place before the Passover, as John presents it?

A Literary Solution?

Verbatim and nearly verbatim material shared among the gospels point inevitably to a literary solution to the problem. There is no adequate explanation for such verbal correspondences apart from the premise that one writer borrowed from another. In fact, this recognition is not modern. As early as the fifth century Augustine proposed that a literary relationship existed among the synoptic gospels. He conjectured that the gospels were written in their present canonical order (i.e., Matthew, Mark, Luke), and that the later gospels had access to the earlier. Throughout the history of New Testament scholarship,[8] explanations for diversity and similarity among the gospels other than a theory of literary relationship have been proposed,[9] but that a literary relationship exists among Matthew, Mark, and Luke has remained the most enduring and plausible explanation.

Two Caveats

Reasonable questions are always justified even concerning the most certain solution. Thus two caveats are in order before proceeding to the current literary solutions.[10] *Caveat one:* the original autographs of the gospels do not exist. Hence, it is not possible to know precisely their original wording. During the early years following their composition, the integrity of the gospels was not respected as highly as it is today. Since the authors of the New Testament did not know they were writing a New Testament, the new writings by early Christians were not initially accorded a status as high as the Jewish Bible, which Jesus and his earliest followers used as their holy books. Thus, Christian scribes felt at liberty to alter and revise the texts that they were copying, or even to harmonize one gospel with another. In short, the texts of the gospels in the first and second centuries were not stable, but continually evolving. A single standard text of the gospels did not exist in antiquity. Each manuscript reads differently. Standardizing the texts of the four gospels is an accomplishment of modern scholarship.

Until recently, the early instability of gospel texts was known only from the assimilation of one gospel to another. For example, Mark 11:26, which is printed in the King James Version but not in the Revised Standard Version and other modern translations, is not considered by scholars who work with the Greek manuscripts (text critics), to have been an original part of the Gospel of Mark, although it does appear in some ancient manuscripts of Mark. Text critics argue that manuscript evidence best supports the idea that Mark 11:26 never was part of the original Gospel of Mark. In the parallel Matthean passage (6:15), however, the verse is unchallenged as a part of the original Gospel of Matthew; it appears in all manuscripts. While it is always possible that the verse was inadvertently omitted from Mark, the evidence argues that the verse (11:26) was added to Mark to harmonize it with Matthew. There are numerous examples of this kind of assimilation of one gospel to another involving whole sentences and, in particular, words and phrases.[11]

The discovery of a fragment of a letter, attributed to Clement of Alexandria, describing a secret Gospel of Mark has provided dramatic new evidence of the early instability of gospel texts.[12] Clement refers to a certain secret gospel, purportedly also written by the author of the original gospel. Clement says the original gospel, written in Rome, was intended by Mark for public use, but the secret gospel, written in Alexandria sometime later, was intended for a more select group of Christians being initiated into advanced "knowledge" in the Alexandrian church. Clement even alludes to a third "Carpocratian" gospel, but denies that it was written by Mark. The letter quotes three excerpts from the secret gospel not present in canonical Mark and also refers to material that could be found in the "Carpocratian" gospel, but is not found in the secret gospel.

Assuming the Clement of Alexandria tradition is genuine, the secret gospel provides significant evidence of the instability of gospel texts. Regardless of whether it was written by the author of the original gospel or not, it attests to three different versions of the Gospel of Mark known to the church in Alexandria at the end of the second century.

Caveat two: No written gospel texts existed between the time of the public career of Jesus and the composition of the Greek gospels—just after the middle of the first century. The first generation of Christians had no written gospel texts; they had only sayings of Jesus and stories about Jesus, which they kept alive in memory and in oral recitation. What Jesus said and did was remembered and repeated in preaching, teaching, debate, and worship contexts. A discussion of the oral period, in which the Jesus traditions were preserved, will be taken up in chapter 7. Here it needs to be noted that oral traditions existed alongside, and in competition with, the written gospels in the latter part of the first century, and even well into the second century.[13] Hence it should not be surprising that scribes harmonized, both inadvertently and deliberately, the later written texts to the still living memory of the oral tradition, particularly in those cases where memory clashed with script.[14]

∞ MARK AS THE FIRST WRITTEN GOSPEL

New Testament scholars generally concur that among the canonical gospels (and *Gospel of Thomas*) Mark was the earliest to be written. Matthew and Luke later used Mark as a written source. The canonical gospels were originally composed in Greek and first used in Greek. The *Gospel of Thomas* was also originally composed in Greek, but exists now only in a later Coptic translation of an earlier Greek version.[15] While the issue is still debated, in the judgment of many (but not all) *Thomas* does not share a literary relationship with the canonical four. *Thomas* does not use them as sources, nor do the canonical four use the *Gospel of Thomas* as a source.[16] *Thomas* did, however, know and use the same oral traditions as the synoptic gospels, and this can account for their similarities. Scholarship lacks a consensus on whether the author of John's gospel knew the synoptic gospels, though most assume that the writer did not draw from them.[17]

A theory of Markan priority accounts for all but one of the classes of material that the synoptic gospels share among themselves (see above pages 53–54). CLASS I (material shared by all three gospels) is material Matthew and Luke have independently taken over from Mark's gospel. Markan material that Matthew alone selected from Mark accounts for the CLASS II material.

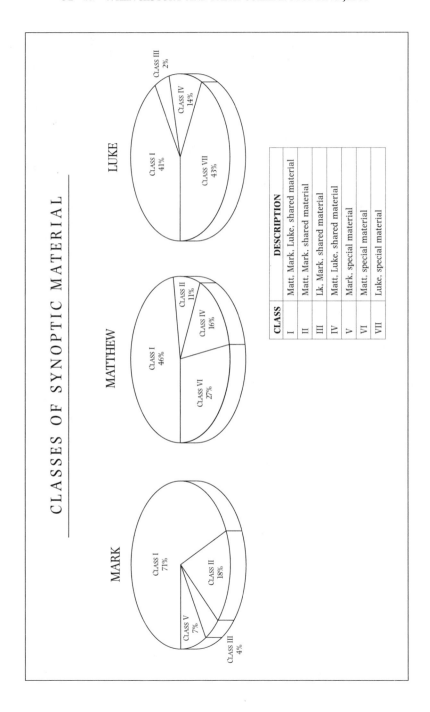

CLASSES OF SYNOPTIC MATERIAL

MARK

CLASS I
71%

CLASS II
18%

CLASS V
7%

CLASS III
4%

MATTHEW

CLASS I
46%

CLASS II
11%

CLASS IV
16%

CLASS VI
27%

LUKE

CLASS I
41%

CLASS III
2%

CLASS IV
14%

CLASS VII
43%

CLASS	DESCRIPTION
I	Matt, Mark, Luke, shared material
II	Matt, Mark, shared material
III	Lk, Mark, shared material
IV	Matt, Luke, shared material
V	Mark, special material
VI	Matt, special material
VII	Luke, special material

CLASS III is Markan material that only Luke used. Matthew and Luke both decided not to use the CLASS V material (the material in Mark only). The special Matthean material (M) (CLASS VI) is Matthew's contribution to what had been taken over from Mark. The special material unique to Luke (L) (CLASS VII) constitutes Luke's contribution. It is not clear whether CLASSES VI and VII were originally written, or if they were material Matthew and Luke garnered out of the oral tradition.

CLASS IV, however, cannot be explained in terms of Matthew's and Luke's borrowing from Mark. The material is not in Mark. It is shared only between Matthew and Luke. That some of the material is almost verbatim in places (e.g., Matt 3:7–10=Luke 3:7–9) is evidence of literary dependency of some sort. Because it seems implausible, at least to most scholars (see below), that a literary relationship existed between Matthew and Luke, an additional, lost source is hypothesized to account for the CLASS IV material. This hypothetical source[18] has never been associated with the name of an early apostle. Scholars refer to it as simply "source." Its usual designation is Q (from the German *Quelle* =source). This hypothetical text will be the subject of chapter 6.

On the basis of Markan priority the gospels of Matthew and Luke become expansions and revisions of the Gospel of Mark. Between the two of them, Matthew and Mark have used most of Mark's material and generally followed Mark's outline, rearranging and adding new material where, and as, it suited their interests. For example, compare Jesus' parables discourse in Mark (Mark 4:1–34) with Matthew's chapter on parables (Matt 13:1–53). Matthew does some rearranging (Mark 4:21=Matt 5:15, Mark 4:22=Matt 10:26, Mark 4:24=Matt 7:2, Mark 4:25=Matt 13:12), but principally adds new material (Matt 13:24–30, 33–53) to expand the discourse. And Luke considerably expands Mark's call and commissioning of the disciples (Mark 3:13–19) by adding new material (cf. Luke 6:12–49). On the other hand, they both occasionally condense Mark's material within individual pericopes (Matt 17:14–21=Mark 9:14–29=Luke 9:37–43a). Two of the larger expansions of Mark's gospel by Matthew and Luke occur at its beginning (Matt 1:1–2:23; Luke 1:1–3:38) and ending (Matt 28:9–20; Luke 24:10–53).

The chart on the facing page illustrates the seven classes of material. The chart on page 86 illustrates the theory of Markan priority.

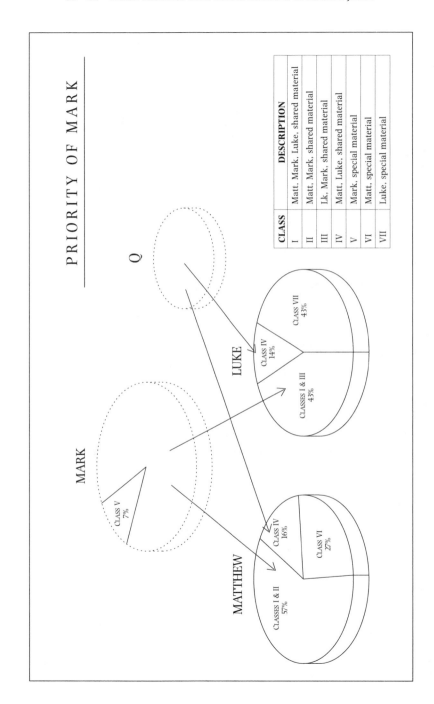

PRIORITY OF MARK

MARK

Q

LUKE

MATTHEW

CLASS V
7%

CLASS IV
16%

CLASSES I & II
57%

CLASS VI
27%

CLASS IV
14%

CLASSES I & III
43%

CLASS VII
43%

CLASS	DESCRIPTION
I	Matt. Mark, Luke, shared material
II	Matt. Mark, shared material
III	Lk. Mark, shared material
IV	Matt. Luke, shared material
V	Mark, special material
VI	Matt. special material
VII	Luke, special material

Why would scholars project a hypothetical source to accommodate the non-Markan material that Matthew and Luke share? Why not simply conclude that a literary relationship existed between them? Then there would be no need for a hypothetical fourth text like Q. This suggestion is plausible to some (see the discussion below). But skeptics argue that the distribution of the CLASS IV material in Matthew and Luke suggests that neither was using the text of the other as a source. In Matthew CLASS IV material appears, for the most part, in the Sermon on the Mount (Matt 5–7). In Luke, on the other hand, many of the sayings in CLASS IV appear as isolated sayings spoken by Jesus on his way to Jerusalem (Luke 9:51–19:44) and in Luke's Sermon on the Plain (Luke 6:17–7:1). On the assumption that Luke saw Matthew it would appear that Luke found the Sermon on the Mount organized as a "speech" of Jesus in Matthew but decided to dismantle it, a conclusion that seems implausible to many. What compelling reason could Luke have had for breaking up the "sermon"? On the other hand, it is possible that Matthew saw Luke and opted to construct the Sermon on the Mount by pulling this Q material from its scattered positions in Luke. But on the assumption that Matthew saw Luke, one must also assume that Matthew also saw Luke's special parables used throughout the gospel and simply decided to ignore most of them, even though Matthew believed that Jesus had only addressed the crowds using parables (Matt 13:34–35).[19] Hence, it appears more likely that Matthew and Luke found the material in a random collection of sayings and each had to decide how they would use it in their respective gospels.

The major weakness of the theory that Matthew and Luke used Mark is the hypothetical source that must be proposed to explain their common material not in Mark. A hypothetical source is always difficult to validate, and hence it weakens the theory. In the mind of many the safest rule to apply in such matters is, the more complicated the explanation, the less convincing the thesis.

The presence of verbatim and nearly verbatim material, however, argues for some literary relationship between Matthew and Luke. If it is not to be explained as a direct literary borrowing, then positing another source seems the only plausible alternative.

∞ MATTHEW AS THE FIRST WRITTEN GOSPEL

Many theories have been proposed to explain the relationship between Matthew, Mark, and Luke. The current competitor to the theory of Markan priority advocates Matthew as the first written gospel, with Luke as second and using Matthew as a source. On this theory Mark was written last and used both Matthew and Luke as sources. This theory accounts for what Matthew, Mark, and Luke have in common (CLASS I): Luke and Mark opted to use the same Matthean material. CLASS II material that only Matthew and Mark share is accommodated by surmising that Luke, for whatever reason, did not use it. Luke took the CLASS IV material (what only Matthew and Luke have in common) from Matthew, and Mark simply decided to omit it. CLASS V (material in Mark alone) constitutes all that Mark adds to what was taken from Matthew and Luke. CLASS VI (material in Matthew alone) is what Luke and Mark both rejected.

Under this theory problems exist with CLASSES III, V, and VII. CLASSES III (Mark and Luke shared material) and VII (Luke special material) is what must ultimately derive from Luke on the basis of this theory, part of which Mark uses (CLASS III) and part Mark does not use (CLASS VII). Approximately 525 verses, a rather sizeable chunk of Luke's gospel, are found in these two classes of material. In order to explain where Luke got it, one must still project the existence of a hypothetical source L. Otherwise it must be assumed that Luke created the material. CLASS V (material in Mark alone) represents all that Mark brought to his editing of the gospels of Matthew and Luke—not a very significant contribution in terms of content. On the basis of Matthew as the first gospel, Mark appears to be an abridgment of both Matthew and Luke. It has sixteen chapters to Matthew's twenty-eight and Luke's twenty-four.

The following chart sets out visually the argument for Matthean priority.

PRIORITY OF MATTHEW

CLASS	DESCRIPTION
I	Matt, Mark, Luke, shared material
II	Matt, Mark, shared material
III	Lk, Mark, shared material
IV	Matt, Luke, shared material
V	Mark, special material
VI	Matt, special material
VII	Luke, special material

MATTHEW — CLASS VI 27%

MARK — CLASSES I, II, III 93%; CLASS V 7%

LUKE — CLASSES I, III 43%; CLASS IV 14%; CLASS VII 43%

L — CLASS VII

There are several weakness to this theory. When Mark was assumed to be the first written gospel, it was necessary to project a hypothetical source to accommodate CLASS IV (material in Matthew and Luke only). The same kind of weakness exists with the theory of Matthean priority. It is still necessary to project a hypothetical source to accommodate the material appearing only in Luke and what is shared only by Luke and Mark (since it came originally from Luke). Again it is not known whether this source is oral or written.

When Matthew is assumed to be first, Mark becomes an abridgment of Matthew and Luke, since Mark is much shorter than Matthew and Luke. But within individual narrative units shared by all three gospels, Mark's narrative is frequently the longer text. This feature may support the argument that Matthew and Luke actually abridged Mark, rather than Mark's shortening Matthew and Luke.[20] To put the matter in another way: why would Mark expand his sources within the individual pericopes, but abbreviate the total narrative in terms of the bulk of material included?

According to this theory, Mark had access to Matthew and Luke and elected to eliminate such things as: narratives about Jesus' birth and genealogy, Matthew's Sermon on the Mount (i.e., teaching material that appears in a different context in Luke), which includes, for example, the Lord's Prayer, the Beatitudes, and the Golden Rule. This theory also has Mark eliminating many parables unique to Luke and Matthew, as well as the resurrection appearances of Jesus that appear at the conclusion of both Matthew and Luke. All Mark adds to this radical abridgment of Matthew and Luke is the CLASS V material—approximately fifty verses appearing throughout Mark. Moreover, Mark finds a high Christology in Matthew and Luke and yet abandons it to portray Jesus in uncomplimentary ways.[21] Further Mark writes in ways that tend to disparage the character of the disciples, contradicting the more positive images presented in Matthew and Luke.[22]

To illustrate the problem that the theory of Matthean priority poses, consider Mark 1:2–11=Matt 3:1–17=Luke 3:1–22 (see also above pages 66–67). Unlike Matthew, Mark gives no specific reason for Jesus' baptism at the hands of John (cf. Matt 3:13–15).

In Matthew Jesus is baptized in accordance with a divine plan. In Luke (and also John), however, the question "Why did John baptize Jesus?" is inappropriate, since John the Baptist is not portrayed as baptizing Jesus (Luke 3:19–22).[23]

Mark never explains why John baptized Jesus, but does tell the reader why John was baptizing. John's baptism in Mark was a "baptism of repentance for the remission of sins" (Mark 1:4—not in Matthew and Luke). The people that John baptized "confessed their sins" (Mark 1:5=Matt 3:6; not in Luke). Hence, given only Mark's text, the logical answer to the question "Why did John baptize Jesus?" is that Jesus came to John along with the crowds of people confessing his sins like they did. And like them he was baptized for the remission of his sins. Matt 3:2 does not include in the summary of John's preaching that John proclaimed a "baptism of repentance for the remission of sins" (Mark 1:6). Matthew does include the statement that people confessing their sins were baptized by John (3:6), but exempts Jesus from this group by specifically stating why Jesus was baptized (3:13–15).

On the basis of the theory that Matthew was written first, it appears that Mark consciously rejected Matthew's explanation for the baptism of Jesus (Matt 3:13–15) and deliberately wrote in such a way that the reader could conclude Jesus was baptized confessing his own sins. Such considerations, of course, do not disprove the theory that Matthew was the first written gospel. They do argue that one must be prepared to give plausible explanations for Mark's thoroughly radical revision of the early Christian tradition he found in Matthew under the theory that Matthew is the first written gospel.

∞

Resolving the literary relationships among the synoptic gospels does not solve every problem, however. Even if we knew without a doubt the compositional sequence, and even if the synoptic problem were "solved," the diversity among the Synoptics and between the Synoptics and John would remain. Nevertheless, identifying the literary relationships among the Synoptics is a step toward a historical explanation for the similarities and differences.

Unraveling the knotty strands of the synoptic problem is no less an enterprise than describing the character of early Christianity in the latter half of the first century. The recognition that a literary relationship of some sort exists among the synoptic gospels forces one to acknowledge that early Christians shaped the tradition at the level of the written texts and raises the question of competing theologies in early Christianity. The synoptic evangelists, the Gospel of John, and the *Gospel of Thomas* were as much "originators" of the tradition as were Jesus and the apostles. Hence readers of the gospels should be sensitive to the tendencies of each evangelist, for such tendencies constitute the evangelist's special interests. Readers who carefully note these distinctives are rewarded with insights into synoptic Christianity in the late first century. How one resolves the literary conundrum of the synoptic problem will determine the nature of synoptic Christianity. If the gospels tell us about Jesus as well as about early Christianity, then some way must be found for sorting out Jesus himself from the interpretations of the evangelists. That question will be taken up in chapter 9.

∞ RECOMMENDED READING AND SOURCES CONSULTED

EHRMAN, B. D. *The Orthodox Corruption of Scripture: The Effect of Early Christological Controversies on the Text of the New Testament.* New York: Oxford, 1993. FARMER, W. R. *The Synoptic Problem: A Critical Analysis.* New York: Macmillan, 1964. SANDERS and DAVIES, *Synoptic Gospels,* 51–119. KÜMMEL, *Introduction to the New Testament,* 38–80. REICKE, BO. *The Roots of the Synoptic Gospels.* Philadelphia: Fortress, 1986. STREETER, B. F. *The Four Gospels: A Study of Christian Origins.* New York: Macmillan, 1926. TYSON, *New Testament and Early Christianity,* 147–58.

∞ ISSUES FOR STUDY AND DISCUSSION

1. Read Matt 4:1–11=Mark 1:12–13=Luke 4:1–13. Explain the order of priority in the literary relationship of these gospels suggested by these readings.

2. Read the following selections from a gospel parallels: Mark 1:23–28=Luke 4:33–37; Mark 12:41–44=Luke 21:1–4. Why do you think these stories were not included in Matthew's gospel. Did Luke get them from Mark or did Mark get them from Luke? Is there another solution?

3. Read Matt 9:9–13=Mark 2:13–17=Luke 5:27–32. Note carefully all similarities and differences. Does the priority of Matthew or the priority of Mark seem most plausible to you? Why?

4. Select two of the passages below; note carefully all similarities and differences and propose a literary theory that best accounts for them:

(a) Matt 12:9–14=Mark 3:1–6=Luke 6:6–11

(b) Matt 8:1–4=Mark 1:40–45=Luke 5:12–16

(c) Matt 9:1–8=Mark 2:1–12=Luke 5:17–26

(d) Matt 9:27–31=Matt 20:29–34=Mark 10:46–52=Luke 18:35–43

(e) Matt 12:38–42=Matt 16:1–4=Mark 8:11–12=Luke 11:16, 29–32

(f) Matt 13:10–17=Mark 4:10–12=Luke 8:9–10, 18b

(g) Matt 26:6–13=Mark 14:3–9=Luke 7:36–50=John 12:1–8

(h) Matt 21:12–13=Mark 11:15–17=Luke 19:45–46=John 2:13–16

5. Select three of the following segments. Why do these passages not appear in Mark?

(a) Matt 5:3–12=Luke 6:20b–23

(b) Matt 6:7–15=Luke 11:1–4

(c) Matt 6:19–21=Luke 12:33–34

(d) Matt 6:25–34=Luke 12:22–32

(e) Matt 7:12=Luke 6:31

(f) Matt 7:24–37=Luke 6:47–49

(g) Matt 10:34–36=Luke 12:51–53

(h) Matt 11:25–27=Luke 10:21–22

(i) Matt 12:43–45=Luke 11:24–26

(j) Matt 8:18–22=Luke 9:57–62

(k) Matt 13:33=Luke 13:20–21

(l) Matt 18:12–14=Luke 15:2–7

6. Select three of the following passages and explain why you think that Matthew and Mark did not include them?

(a) Luke 7:11–17

(b) Luke 13:10–17

(c) Luke 14:1–6

(d) Luke 14:7–14

(e) Luke 15:8–10

(f) Luke 15:11–32

(g) Luke 16:1–9

(h) Luke 18:1–8

(i) Luke 19:1–10

(j) Luke 23:6–16

7. Read Mark 3:19b–21: Why did Matthew and Luke not include this segment?

8. *Select two of the following and suggest reasons why you think that Luke did not include them?*

(a) Matt 14:22–33=Mark 6:45–52=John 6:16–21

(c) Matt 15:29–31=Mark 7:31–37

(b) Matt 15:21–28=Mark 7:24–30

(d) Matt 21:20–22=Mark 11:20–26

9. *Read Matt 18:19–20; Matt 20:1–16; Matt 25:31–46. Why did Mark and Luke not include these?*

10. *Suggest some reasons for the differences among the endings to the synoptic gospels: Matt 28:1–20=Mark 16:1–8=Luke 24:1–53.*

6

A LOST SAYINGS GOSPEL?

Chapter 5 showed that the CLASS IV material (material that Matthew and Luke share, but Mark does not) derived from a lost document used as a source by Matthew and Luke. "Lost" is not exactly the correct word to describe it. It must be reconstructed from material common to Matthew and Luke and is better regarded, therefore, as a hypothetical source. Apart from the agreements between Matthew and Luke in the CLASS IV material, there is no evidence that Q ever existed. Those who think Matthew and Luke used a written source, however, argue that Q clearly does "exist," at least in part, in the material shared only by Matthew and Luke, and that it is certainly "lost," since no ancient manuscripts of Q exist, as they do for the canonical and other noncanonical gospels. If Matthew and Luke have preserved passages from a lost sayings source, as a majority of New Testament scholars now think, then its recovery is a spectacular feat of New Testament criticism. Q would be nothing less than the earliest list of the sayings of Jesus.

Q is called a *sayings* gospel because, like the *Gospel of Thomas* (which was given the title "gospel" in antiquity), it also does not tell a story. Q and the *Gospel of Thomas* are simply collections of sayings and stories by and about Jesus (and John the Baptist); neither is a narrative with a beginning, middle, and end. There is neither story nor plot. In fact scholars do not even agree generally upon what organizating principle controls each collection. Q has been called a "sayings gospel" because it belongs to the same genre as the *Gospel of Thomas* and in order to distinguish it from the narrative gospel genre.

∞ RECONSTRUCTING THE LOST SAYINGS GOSPEL Q

Since the turn of the century, scholars have identified Q as the material common to Matthew and Luke but not Mark. In some cases this material agrees nearly word-for-word in Greek (like Matt 3:7–10=Luke 3:7–9). In other cases it follows closely but is not verbatim (like Matt 5:46–47=Luke 6:32–33). To highlight the similarities and differences scholars set such passages in parallel columns. Differences are italicized in the passage below.

Matthew 3:7–10	Luke 3:7–9
"You brood of vipers! Who warned you to flee from the wrath to come? Bear *fruit* that *befits* repentance, and do not *presume* to say to yourselves, 'We have Abraham as our father'; for I tell you God is able from these stones to raise up children to Abraham. Even now the ax is laid to the root of the trees; every tree therefore that does not bear good fruit is cut down and thrown into the fire."	"You brood of vipers! Who warned you to flee from the wrath to come? Bear *fruits* that *befit* repentance, and do not *begin* to say to yourselves, 'We have Abraham as our father'; for I tell you God is able from these stones to raise up children to Abraham. *Also* even now the ax is laid to the root of the trees; every tree therefore that does not bear good fruit is cut down and thrown into the fire."

On the one hand, this saying is virtually the same in the Greek of Matthew and Luke, as one would suppose from the English translations. The two passages are so similar in this case that only the differences need be noted. The narrative introductions to the sayings (Matt 3:7a=Luke 3:7a), on the other hand, are remarkably different. Such diversity in the literary frames of sayings has led scholars to conclude that Q was simply a collection of sayings having no literary introductions. Matthew and Luke found this saying in the Q collection, where it was identified as a saying of John the Baptist. Hence each had to provide it a narrative context, and each elected to do it differently. Not all sayings in Q correspond as closely as this, however. The passages below share some verbal similarities as well as a good deal of difference; yet both have similar structures.

Matthew 5:46–47	Luke 6:32–33
For if *you love* **those who love you,** what reward have *you?* Do not **even the** tax collectors do the same? **And if** *you* salute only *your* brethren, what more are *you* doing than others? Do not **even the** Gentiles **do the same?**	And if *you love* **those who love you,** what credit is that to *you?* For **even the** sinners love those who love them. **And if** *you* do good to those who do good to *you,* what credit is that to *you?* For **even the** sinners **do the same.**

The bold faced terms are verbatim in Greek; italicized words indicate a different form of the same Greek word. The versatility of Greek allows it to say the same thing using synonyms and different inflections of the same word. For example, "you love" in Matthew's Greek appears as ἀγαπήσητε while in Luke it appears as ἀγαπᾶτε. They are translated the same, however. Yet in spite of the differences between the two sayings they appear to be unique performances of the same saying. For example, the distinction between "what reward have you?" (Matt 5:46a) and "what credit is that to you?" (Luke 6:32) is not significant. It might be argued that tax collectors (Matthew) and sinners (Luke) are quite different, but in some ways they are similar. In the first century a tax collector was regarded as a sinner; hence Matthew's reading is more specific, while Luke's is more general. The same may be said for Gentiles (Matthew) and sinners (Luke).

It is not certain whose performance of the saying, Matthew's or Luke's, more faithfully reflects the way Q read. In general, scholars tend to favor Luke's sequence of the sayings as more faithfully reproducing the order of Q, and to signal this they cite the Q text by the chapter and verse numeration of Luke's gospel. It is not always the case, however, that Luke's readings best reflect the Q text, and hence each situation must be carefully analyzed. In this case it is simply not possible to know precisely what Q read. But the close verbal and structural agreements between the sayings have convinced scholars that the verses were originally available to Matthew and Luke in a written source. Both evangelists adapted the saying in their individual narratives and that accounts for their differences.

∞ RECONSTRUCTING Q LETTER BY LETTER

Some scholars are so convinced of Q's existence they are attempting to recover the text of Q (which some refer to as "PapQ," for papyrus Q)[1] by a detailed comparison of the Q saying (in Greek), reproducing only the Greek letters that Matthew and Luke share. It is argued that this analysis results in the reconstruction of a partial text of Q, not unlike fragmentary ancient papyrus manuscripts that have deteriorated because of the ravages of time, climate, worms, etc. For example, using this method the *certain* vestiges of PapQ 6:32–33 would look like the following in Greek:
PapQ 6:32–33

[   ]ε[   ] ἀγαπ[   ] τοὺς ἀγαπῶντας ὑμᾶς [   ]α [   ] ἐ[ ];
[   ] καὶ οἱ [   ]ω[   ]ι το[   ]αὐτο[   ]σιν[ ]καὶ ἐὰν ἀ[   ]ε
[   ]ε[   ]ν[ ]ο[ ]ὑμ[ ]ν[   ]ι[   ]; [   ]καὶ[
]οἱ τὸ αὐτὸ ποιοῦσιν[

According to this hypothetical reconstruction, these Greek letters are all that survive of Q 6:32–33 from the "papyrus document" Matthew and Luke are thought to have used along with Mark as a source for their gospels. The gaps between the brackets represent what has been lost from PapQ due to the editing of Matthew and Luke. Of course, the complete original text of Q may well be preserved in either Matthew or Luke, but the words and letters they share most probably reflect the Q text. Or, put another way, they represent what surely must have come from Q—on the theory that Q actually existed as an ancient papyrus document. The material lacking in Q is being restored from Matthew and Luke through detailed analysis and scholarly debate. The common Greek letters, however, represent the irreducible minimum of Q.[2]

∞ THE ORDER OF SAYINGS IN Q?

Since Matthew and Luke tended to extract sayings from Q and use them in different locations in their gospels, establishing an original order, or sequence, of sayings in Q would seem to be impossible. For example, there are two versions of the Lord's Prayer: Matt 6:9–13=Luke 11:2–4. A great deal of similarity exists in the way Matthew and Luke report the prayer, yet Matthew includes it as one of the sayings of the Sermon on the Mount (Matt 5–7), while Luke includes it as one of the sayings of Jesus spoken on his final journey to Jerusalem (Luke 9:51–19:44). Luke has a Sermon on the Plain (Luke 6:12–7:1) where the Lord's Prayer could have been situated to match Matthew's Sermon on the Mount placement. Also Matthew has a short final trip of Jesus to Jerusalem (19:1b–20:34) where the prayer could have been placed to correspond to Luke. Since Q had no narrative framework to guide either evangelist, however, they simply included the prayer where it made most sense to each gospel author.

The situation is not completely hopeless, however. Q scholars note that there are five Q pericopae occurring in the same order in both Matthew and Luke: John's preaching, the baptism of Jesus, the temptation of Jesus, the Sermon on the Mount/ Plain, and the narrative of the centurion's servant. With this common order as a basis, Q scholars have generally agreed that the Lukan order, in the main, best represents the original order of Q.[3] There are places, however, where Luke diverges from Q, and Matthew is thought to preserve the original Q order, as for example, the sequence of the temptations in Matt 4:1–11=Luke 4:1–13. In this case, as well as others, the Matthean order is preferred over Luke's.[4]

There are several reasons Q scholars are interested in recovering the original order of Q, all of them related. First, it is an interesting question. Critical study has led to the positing of a second source used by Matthew and Luke, and scholars want to know as much as they can about the source. If it actually was a written source, then the order of its sayings is important, because sequence implies an interpretation. In the second place, firming up an order of the Q sayings gives substance to what is admittedly a hypothetical "document." That is one reason that Q has been dubbed "PapQ." The designation claims for Q the same status as any fragmentary papyrus manuscript that must be restored after discovery. The same principles and techniques involved in the establishment of a critical text for newly discovered manuscripts are also by analogy claimed for Q. And thus Q studies appear a little less hypothetical. A determination of Q's order leads to understanding Q's theology is the final reason. In sayings collections, the arrangement of sayings suggests their scribal interpretation in much the same way the context of sayings in the Sermon on the Mount or the *Gospel of Thomas* leads a reader to understand sayings in a certain way. The same would be true for Q, if its order could be determined. In short, what is at stake in Q's order is the character of an earlier stage of Christian history.

⠶ Q OVERLAPS?

Q scholars think that Mark and Q have in some few instances independently selected and used the same material. Hence they overlap in the use of that material. In those instances scholars assume that Mark used material incorporated also into Q, and that Matthew and Luke followed Q rather than Mark. But why not just assume that Mark was the source and simply dispense with Q as a source for that material? In some cases the overlaps seem fairly obvious. For example, the temptation of Jesus is preserved in Matthew (4:1–11), Mark (1:12–13), and Luke (4:1–13). But Mark's report is so brief, and Matthew and Luke are so similar, that it is difficult to resist the conclusion that Matthew and Luke are using a written source other than Mark.

On the other hand, the baptism of Jesus as reported in Matthew (3:16–17), Mark (1:9–11), and Luke (3:21–22) is quite similar in all the three gospels, and the agreements of Matthew and Luke against Mark so few, it raises the question: why could not Matthew and Luke simply have gotten this report from Mark? Why should one project a hypothetical source to explain the common similarities between Matthew and Luke in this instance? One reason that some Q scholars include the baptism pericope as a part of Q is that they want to explain why Matthew and Luke share agreements in Greek usage (although they are few) not in Mark. Another reason is that the temptation narratives presuppose a "Son of God" Christology, and Q therefore needs a narrative, something like the baptism of Jesus, to set out this feature more definitely.[5] In any case, Q scholars generally agree that Q contained a temptation narrative but divide on whether or not it contained a baptism account.

∞ THE CHARACTER OF THE LOST SAYINGS GOSPEL Q

What kind of a "text" was Q? What did it contain specifically? When was it written? What kind of an author, or community, might have put it together? Even though Q is a hypothetical construct from the shared materials in Matthew and Luke, Q scholars are confident enough of its actual existence in the past to treat it like any other ancient document.

The Contents of Q

A recent renewal of interest in the sayings gospel Q since the middle 1980s has sparked a number of publications describing the contents of Q. In this section the passages in John Kloppenborg's reconstruction of Q are listed by Luke's chapter and verse numeration.[6] The parentheses indicate passages thought likely to have come from Q, but in Kloppenborg's judgment they are not as certain as the other material in the list.

Q 3:7–9	John's Preaching of Repentance
Q 3:16b–17	John's Preaching of the Coming One
Q 4:1–13	The Temptations of Jesus
Q 6:20b–23, (24–26)	Blessings and Woes
Q 6:27–33, (34–35b), 35c	On Retaliation
Q 6:36–37b, (37c–38b), 38c	On Judging
Q 6:39b–40	Blind Guides, Teachers and Pupils
Q 6:41–42	On Hypocrisy
Q 6:43–45	Good and Evil Men
Q 6:46–49	The Parable of the Builders
Q 7:1b–2, (3–5), 6–10	The Centurion's Son
Q 7:18–19, (20), 22–23	John's Inquiry
Q 7:24–28	Jesus' Eulogy of John
Q 16:16	The Kingdom Suffers Violence
Q 7:31–35	The Children in the Agora
Q 9:57–60, (61–62)	Three Followers of Jesus
Q 10:2–12	The Mission Speech
Q 10:13–15	Woes on Galilean Towns
Q 10:16	The Authority of Missionaries
Q 10:21–22	Thanksgiving for Revelation
Q 10:23b–24	Blessing on the Eyewitnesses
Q 11:2–4	The Lord's Prayer

Q 11:9–13	Confidence in Prayer
Q 11:14–18a, 19–20, (21–22), 23	The Beelzebul Incident
Q 11:24–26	The Return of the Evil Spirit
Q (11:27–28)	True Blessedness
Q 11:16, 29–32	The Sign of Jonah
Q 11:33–35, (36)	The Lamp and the Eye
Q 11:39b–44, 46–52	Woes against the Pharisees
Q 12:2–3	Hidden and Revealed
Q 12:4–7	Appropriate Fear
Q 12:8–9	On Confessing Jesus
Q 12:10	Blasphemy of the Spirit
Q 12:11–12	The Spirit's Assistance
Q (12:13–14, 16–21)	Foolish Possessions
Q 12:22–31	Earthly Cares
Q 12:33–34	Heavenly Treasure
Q 12:39–40	The Householder and the Thief
Q 12:42b–46	Faithful and Unfaithful Servants
Q 12:(49), 51–53	Fire and Division on Earth
Q 12:54–56	Signs of the Times
Q 12:57–59	Agreeing with an Accuser
Q 13:18–21	The Mustard and the Leaven
Q 13:24, (25), 26–27	The Narrow Gate and the Closed Door
Q 13:28–30	Gentiles in the Kingdom
Q 13:34–35	Lament over Jerusalem
Q 14:11/18:14b	Exalting the Humble
Q 14:16–24	The Great Supper
Q 14:26–27; 17:33	Being Disciples
Q 14:34–35	Savorless Salt
Q 15:4–7	The Lost Sheep
Q (15:8–10)	The Lost Coin
Q 16:13	God and Mammon
Q 16:16–18	The Kingdom, the Law, and Divorce
Q 17:1b–2	On Scandals
Q 17:3b–4	Forgiveness
Q 17:6b	On Faith
Q 17:23–24, 26–27 (28–29), 30, 34–35, 37b	The Coming of the Son of Man
Q 19:12–13, 15b–26	The Parable of the Talents
Q 22:28–30	Judging Israel

Is Q a Complete Gospel?

The quick response to the question is how could anyone possibly know, since we have only what Matthew and Luke together but independently decided to incorporate into their narratives. But Q's character as a collection of sayings with no narrative framework has led Q scholars to conclude that Q, like the *Gospel of Thomas*, did not tell a story as did the canonical gospels. In fact, the discovery of the *Gospel of Thomas* in 1945 was a spectacular confirmation of the scholarly judgment that sayings gospels like Q had existed. If Q is a sayings collection with no narrative plot, then it clearly is "lacking" material that readers of the canonical gospels regard as integral parts of the gospel genre, although it is unlikely that the compiler of Q thought anything was lacking. For example, Q includes neither a birth nor a passion narrative (compare the passion narrative, Mark 14–16, and parallels): that is, Q does not describe the virgin birth or Jesus' suffering, death, and resurrection. Since Q (like *Gospel of Thomas*) lacks a narrative about the passion, the author was apparently able to conceptualize Jesus and his career apart from his death and resurrection. If Q was a sayings collection, at most it might have contained sayings on the cross, but nothing in Q indicates this. It certainly did not have a narrative of Jesus' crucifixion.

In part, it may also be said that certain of the canonical gospels "lack" material. While they all include a passion narrative, Mark and John apparently did not find it necessary to use birth narratives to describe Jesus—because they do not use them. In other words, early Christians described Jesus' public career in different ways. For some (like *Gospel of Thomas* and Q) virgin birth, crucifixion, and resurrection were apparently not essential components of their gospel. In the *Gospel of Thomas* and Q, Jesus is presented more as a teacher of wisdom than as a suffering servant.

The Date of Q

Since Q is a (hypothetical) source used by Matthew and Luke, it follows that it must have been written prior to their composition. Matthew and Luke were composed and published after Mark sometime after 70 C.E. The usual dates are between 80 and 100. It follows, therefore, that Q was composed sometime prior to 80 C.E.

Recent work on Q, however, has argued that Q went through several editions, and Q scholars have thus posited different layers to Q: the sayings of Q existed initially (1) as independent sayings, which* (2) were gathered into a primitive collection, which (3) later was edited and revised.[7] Originally Q was a collection of wisdom and eschatological sayings that were later revised by an editor with apocalyptic tendencies.[8] Hence because of its lengthy literary history, and its "primitive" character (i.e., as a collection of sayings), scholars usually project the date of its final editing as 50–60 C.E. The original Q collection is reasoned to have been much earlier than the version used by Matthew and Luke; some scholars think that it was virtually contemporary with the earliest followers of Jesus.[9]

Author and Community?

Scholars work backwards from the reconstructed Q text to the author, and theorize about the Q community by asking the following kind of question: What kind of author or community might have produced such a text? It is assumed that the character and concerns of the sayings in Q reveal the interests of those earliest followers of Jesus. These early Christians selected from among those things they heard Jesus say (or were told that he had said, or thought that he had said) what they found to be significant for understanding themselves and their post-Jesus world.[10]

It is not possible to identify a historical individual who produced the nucleus of the collection, and for that reason scholars talk about the profile of the "community" responsible for the sayings collection. Sayings collections are quite flexible. Each new "publication" can easily drop or add sayings to reflect changed community interest. The sayings of Q suggest the community was rather different from the later more organized churches producing the canonical gospels. Sketched in broad outlines, the Q community is generally thought by Q scholars to be a group existing on the margins of first-century society, probably in the regions of northern Galilee and southwest Syria (cf. Q 10:13–15 and 13:34–35). They constituted a world-rejecting, itinerant gathering of people that lived close to the edge of human existence, frequently lacking the necessities of life.[11] Such a loose gathering differs from the later Hellenistic church communities, who consciously thought of themselves as citizens of the Roman state and who belonged to ecclesiastical organizations with specific religious rites and clergy.

Jesus in the Sayings Gospel Q

What sort of portrait of Jesus emerges from Q?[12] What would a first-century reader think of Jesus after reading Q? A modern reader faces the same kind of problem with Q that exists with the *Gospel of Thomas.* Q is not a narrative and, like the *Gospel of Thomas*, it is thought to have several layers of tradition. Hence the character of Jesus must be extrapolated from the sayings themselves. The following description profiles an image of Jesus emerging from the Q versions used by Matthew and Luke.

There is apparently a close connection between the movement inaugurated by John the Baptist and Jesus. John announces Jesus as the anticipated "stronger one," whose baptism differed from John's own water baptism in that Jesus' baptism was characterized by "holy spirit and fire" (3:16b). He was to sort the "chaff" from the "wheat" (3:17)—in other words, his career would be controversial and divisive. Jesus honored John, but at the same time distanced himself from the baptizer (7:24–28; 16:16). Indeed, John had taken an ascetic path, whereas Jesus lived in such a way that he could be described as a glutton and a drunk (7:31–35).

An initial spiritual experience was formative for Jesus' mission. He bested the devil in a debate over the character of his work. His responses to the devil's challenges set the tone for a lifestyle that disdained the "things" of the world (4:1–13; 10:4; 12:13–14, 16–21). He identified himself with the poor, the hungry, the disenfranchised (6:20b–23), and the marginalized of society (15:4–10), to whom he thought the kingdom of God truly belonged (6:20b). He rejected the rich (6:24–26) and the religious authorities (11:39b–44, 46–52).

It is not clear that he invited followers into his company, but people clearly followed him (9:57–62). He alluded to them as "prophets" (11:49) and "workers" (10:2), rather than "disciples" (but cf. 6:20a). He set these prophets upon an itinerant mission (10:2–12) into a hostile world (10:3, 10), and they were clearly expected to exacerbate that hostility against them (12:49–53). He told them to sell everything they had and give it all away (12:33); and hence they should take nothing with them on the mission (10:4). They were to go as indigent "workers in the Lord's harvest," living off the hospitality offered them (10:4–12). They were not ascetic, however, but were commanded to eat whatever was set before them (10:7–8). They were commissioned to "heal the sick and announce the nearness of the kingdom of God" (10:9).

The Jesus of Q taught complete nonviolence (6:29), love of enemies (6:27–28, 32–35), humility (14:11; 18:14b), and unlimited forgiveness (17:3–4). He rejected material possessions as having no value at all (6:30, 35), and taught his followers to rely on God for their daily needs (11:3; 12:22–31). Whatever they needed would be provided; they had only to ask (11:9–13). He also taught his followers to be merciful and nonjudgmental (6:36–38). He held up before them a radical faith that would enable them to do what was humanly impossible (17:6). This is the "way" to become a true child of God (6:35).

Although he condemned the Pharisees and Torah lawyers (11:46–48, 52), he affirmed tithing (11:42) and the Torah (16:17), yet he disagreed with Torah's teaching that divorce was permitted (16:18; cf. Deut 24:1–4). He had harsh words for hypocrites who criticized others and were unaware of their own failings (6:41–42).

Q's Jesus accepted John's affirmation that he (Jesus) was the "stronger one who was coming," and offered as evidence his miraculous deeds and the fact that his mission was to the poor (7:18–23). Jesus, however, referred to himself the "one who comes in the name of the Lord" (13:35), and perhaps also "Son of Man" (7:31–35; 9:58; but cf. 12:8–10; 17:23–24, 26–29 where "Son of Man" may be a figure other than Jesus). He claimed a special understanding of God that the sages of the world did not have (10:21) and announced the nearness of God's kingdom, i.e., his reign (7:28; 9:62; 10:9; 11:20; 12:31; 13:18–21, 29), claiming that his exorcisms brought God's reign near (11:14–23, 24–26). He seemed to think of the kingdom in terms of Israel's faith that they were the true people of God (22:28–30). He divided the world into two camps: those with him and those against him (11:23); the latter he referred to as "this (evil) generation" (7:31; 11:29, 32; 11:51).

His preaching polarized the communities he visited (12:49–53; 13:24, 28–30; 14:26–27; 17:33), for he tolerated no half-way commitment to his mission and indigent lifestyle (16:13). In no uncertain terms (10:12; 12:4–7, 8–12) he condemned those who did not respond to his message. When people asked him for a sign to validate himself, he offered only the sign of "Jonah" (11:16, 29), by which he meant his preaching and the response to it (11:16, 29–32).

∞

Q is the product of scientific methodology, logic, and the most probable deductions from the available evidence. But if the scholarly reconstruction of Q is indeed the recovery of a lost collection of Jesus' sayings antedating the canonical gospels, it is still only one other way that early Christians viewed Jesus. The striking similarities and equally obvious differences among these diverging portraits (see chapter 3 above) highlight the fundamental problem of recovering precise dimensions of the historical figure behind them all. For scholars, Q is a bridge over an embarrassing gap in the corpus of early Christian literature. It is a long jump from Jesus (ca. 30 C.E.) to the first extant early Christian gospel (ca. 70 C.E.). Packed into that period is the significant shift of early Christianity from Jewish sect to independent Hellenistic religion. With the recovery of Q, the way back to the historical Jesus is illuminated more clearly and the way forward to the exalted Christ of the early Christian gospels is made more understandable. Nevertheless, while Q may take us closer to the lifetime of Jesus chronologically, it is still one more interpretation.

The fundamental question remains: is it possible to penetrate through these early Christian literary interpretations and clarify the character of the historical man? The final chapter describes methods used by scholars for breaking through these literary barriers, which both facilitate and hinder the quest.

∞ RECOMMENDED READING AND SOURCES CONSULTED

JACOBSON, A. D. *The First Gospel: An Introduction to Q.* Sonoma, Calif.: Polebridge, 1992. KLOPPENBORG, J. S. *The Formation of Q: Trajectories in Ancient Wisdom Collections.* Studies in Antiquity and Christianity; Philadelphia: Fortress, 1987. KLOPPENBORG, J. S. *Q Parallels: Synopsis, Critical Notes and Concordance.* Sonoma Calif.: Polebridge, 1988. KLOPPENBORG, MEYER, et al. *Q-Thomas Reader.* KOESTER, HELMUT. *Ancient Christian Gospels: Their History and Development.* Philadelphia: Trinity Press International, 1990.

MACK, BURTON L. *The Lost Gospel: The Book of Q and Christian Origins* (San Francisco: HarperSanFrancisco, 1993). ROBINSON, JAMES M. *The Jesus of the Sayings Gospel Q* (Occasional Papers of the Institute for Antiquity and Christianity 28; Claremont, Calif.: Institute for Antiquity and Christianity, 1993). STREETER, *Four Gospels*, 271–92. VAAGE, LEIF E. *Galilean Upstarts: Jesus' First Followers According to Q.* Valley Forge, Penn.: Trinity Press International, 1994.

∞ ISSUES FOR STUDY AND DISCUSSION

1. *Compare Kloppenborg's reconstruction of Q to Matthew, Mark, Luke, or John. What does Q not have that the other source does?*

2. *On the basis of the type of sayings found in Q, in what do you think the Q community was most interested?*

3. *Kloppenborg has excluded some Q sayings that others accept. Select one of the following and explain why you think that it should be included or excluded from Q.*

    a. Matt 3:1–6=Luke 3:1–4
    b. Matt 21:31–32=Luke 7:29–30
    c. Matt 3:13–17=Luke 3:21–22
    d. Matt 12:11–12=Luke 14:5

4. *In what ways are Q and the* Gospel of Thomas *similar, and why is it important to note the similarities?*

5. *Why do you think a scholar would assign Luke 11:27–28 to Q when it has no parallel in Matthew?*

6. *Why do you think the parable of the Lost Coin (Luke 15:8–10) is thought to be a Q text, although it has no parallel in Matthew? Do you agree with this rationale?*

7. *Compare and contrast Q's Jesus with the concept of Jesus emerging in one of the following:*

    a. Mark
    b. Luke
    c. John

8. *Select two of the following. Which best represents the extant text of Q? Why?*

    a. Matt 3:11–12=Luke 3:16b–17
    b. Matt 15:13–14, 24–25=Luke 6:39–40

c. Matt 11:4–6=Luke 7:22–23
d. Matt 11:16–19=Luke 7:31–35
e. Matt 8:18–22=Luke 9:57–62

9. Summarize the reasons that scholars think Matthew and Luke used a lost sayings gospel.

10. Read through the sayings of Q as reconstructed by Kloppenborg and develop your own description of one of the following:

a. Jesus
b. The Q Community

7

FROM ORAL TRADITION TO WRITTEN GOSPEL

The early Christian gospels, *the Gospel of Thomas* and Q (if the CLASS IV material actually did exist independently as a written text in antiquity), are the principal avenues of access to Jesus of Nazareth. But they are not neutral accesses. Rather these early Christian texts are theologically slanted narratives dating almost a generation after the events they describe. How does a modern reader know that anything they tell us originated forty years or so earlier with the historical Jesus? Or, to put the matter differently: How was the actual life experience of the events kept alive in the period between the end of Jesus' public career and the later writing of the gospels? Modern scholars theorize what Jesus said and did survived in fragmentary form in the collective memories of individual Christians shortly after the events. What Jesus said and did passed from events experienced in public life in the 30s into events remembered and subsequently orally described as the occasion arose in the next forty or so years. Later in the latter half of the first century these were transformed into written gospels. That is to say:

from actual events to an oral tradition about the events into written descriptions of the events.

There is even an early Christian tradition actually describing the middle term (oral tradition) in the equation stated above. Papias, in the first half of the second century,[1] described a period of time, between Jesus and the writing of the gospels, when traditions about Jesus were remembered and passed on by the earliest Christians. This means that stories about Jesus, his words, and reports of what he did were passed orally to those who had not known him during his public career. What Papias reported about this period of time in the case of the Gospel of Mark is worth examining a little more closely:

> [John] the Elder used to say this also: Mark became the interpreter of Peter and he wrote down accurately, but not in order, as much as he remembered of the sayings and doings of the Lord. For he was not a hearer or follower of the Lord, but afterwards, as I said, of Peter, who adapted his teachings to the needs of the moment and did not make an ordered exposition of the sayings of the Lord. And so Mark made no mistake when he thus wrote down some things as he remembered them; for he made it his especial care to omit nothing of what he heard and to make no false statement therein.[2]

The quotation suggests: (1) Mark wrote what Peter told him; (2) Mark wrote sometime after the discussion(s) with Peter, since Mark wrote "as much as he remembered" (i.e., he only wrote "some" things);[3] (3) what Mark wrote was not "in order";[4] (4) Mark "interpreted" what Peter told him; (5) even Peter had interpreted (i.e., "adapted his teachings to the needs of the moment") what he told Mark; (6) what Peter told Mark was not "an ordered exposition"; (7) what was transmitted between Peter and Mark were sayings and deeds, not a complete narrative. This scenario, extrapolated from Eusebius, is virtually identical to the way critical scholars describe the preserving of the Jesus tradition today.

Oral transmitting of the sayings and deeds of Jesus among the early Christians continued well into the second century. Even after the writing of the gospels, Papias himself continued to rely upon oral reports (i.e., the "tradition") about Jesus that he received from those later followers who were disciples of the "holy apostles" (i.e., the earliest followers of Jesus).[5]

Evidence of a period when sayings and deeds of Jesus survived only in the memory of the church can also be found in the New Testament. In the prologue to the Gospel of Luke the author specifies the primary sources for the gospel as being oral (Luke 1:2, "delivered" to us from eyewitnesses) but also written (Luke 1:1, "many have undertaken to compile a narrative"). Paul also referred to certain Jesus traditions that he had "received" and "delivered" to others (1 Cor 15:3–7), and he also knows, apparently through this oral source,[6] certain sayings of Jesus (1 Cor 7:10–11; 9:14; in 1 Cor 14:37 Paul alludes to a saying of the Lord but does not quote it).[7] Whether Paul had met Jesus is uncertain. Paul's information about Jesus is thought to have come through oral reports. His letters suggest that he had little knowledge about the circumstances of Jesus' historical life. Rather they show a keener interest in the resurrected Lord of Christian faith.

The gospels portray Jesus as an oral teacher. There is no hint that he ever committed his teaching to writing. The only description of his early training (John 7:15) characterizes him as "knowing letters" but not being formally trained. According to the gospels, he commissioned his disciples to proclaim their message orally (cf., e.g., Mark 6:11–12; Matt 10:5–8; Luke 9:1–2), but scribal activities, such as the production of books, are not mentioned, nor is there any indication that Jesus required his followers to memorize his teaching.

Hence New Testament scholars project a period between the public career of Jesus and the writing of the first gospels when the Jesus traditions (i.e., his sayings, stories about him, and his deeds) survived only in the memory of his followers. When the church turned to writing to preserve this information, the written gospels did not immediately replace the oral tradition. Even into the second century the oral tradition remained alongside the written texts as an alternate source and a subtle competitor to the written gospels.

Did the oral transmission of the Jesus traditions have any effect on the tradition? Was the church's memory influenced by its changing cultural situation? To answer these questions a reader needs to know how oral traditions work. Then the influence of the oral period on the tradition can be better assessed.

∞ HOW ORAL TRADITIONS WORK

Anthropological Studies of Oral Literature

Since the first-century world (where oral traditions about Jesus originated and were transmitted) no longer exists, some scholars investigate contemporary preliterate societies, or societies in which they find recognizable collections of oral literature (such as folk tales, folklore, and folk music) existing alongside written literature. Such studies, when applied to ancient traditional literature, previously oral but now written, assume that the principles governing the transmission of oral traditions are much the same in every culture and period.[8] This modern anthropological approach to the study of oral traditions in preliterate societies has previously been little used in the study of the New Testament.[9]

Classical Studies and Orality

Milman Parry in the late 1920s began investigating the oral roots to Homer's *Iliad* and *Odyssey*.[10] Parry argued that these texts were traditional oral literature composed by a school of poets who drew on certain stock expressions and formulae rather than on the work of one individual poet. He then turned his attention to contemporary illiterate bards in Yugoslavia to show that they worked in a similar fashion. These modern oral poets composed their poetry by drawing on a traditional store of formulae and themes. When they acquired a song from another singer and performed it, they did not perform exactly the same song, but the new song was different in numerous ways. Thus their song was a new performance rather than a repetition of the song they had acquired. Parry showed that the song performed by the contemporary bard was greatly influenced by the audience and occasion, and that exact memorization was not a part of the bards' methodology. Later studies have challenged and modified, but not discredited, the work of Parry.[11]

Oral Tradition and Form Criticism in
New Testament Studies

Hermann Gunkel, a scholar of the Hebrew Bible, described the book of Genesis as religious folk traditions that had circulated in small oral units before being written down.[12] Influenced by Gunkel's studies, New Testament scholars began to analyze the gospels under the assumption that they also had been compiled out of traditional oral units. The three pioneering works in applying this method to the New Testament are Martin Dibelius, *From Tradition to Gospel* (1st German ed., 1919), Karl Ludwig Schmidt, *Der Rahmen der Geschichte Jesu* (1919),[13] and Rudolf Bultmann, *The History of the Synoptic Tradition* (1st German ed., 1921).

This method of study was called *Formgeschichte*, literally "the [study of the] history of forms," but it was translated into English as "form criticism." Under the influence of Gunkel's success, Dibelius, and later Bultmann, worked through the New Testament identifying the traditional literary forms that the evangelists received and adapted; Schmidt analyzed the literary frames that the evangelists were thought to have created to enclose the traditional oral units. Before being applied to the biblical literature, the method had been developed in the study of German and Scandinavian folklore and folk tales. Through the years Bultmann's study has been the more influential of the two. These earlier studies were not based on a broad analysis of the way oral traditions work. To a large extent they assumed that the gospel material had been preserved orally and then they proceeded to describe the process of transmission in the oral period on the basis of an analysis of the synoptic gospels.[14] In other words, they derived the principles of oral transmission from the written forms of the synoptic literature. None of the studies contained a section on the principles of oral transmission as such.[15]

For students of form criticism, the "church" was the preserver of the Jesus traditions. That meant the Jesus tradition began in Aramaic-speaking Palestine following the Easter experience of the church. After early Christians came to believe in the resurrection of Jesus,[16] they tended to view all aspects of the Jesus tradition in the light of their belief that God had raised Jesus from the dead.

Consequently that belief influenced what they remembered and how they remembered it (cf. John 2:22).

In its earliest phase, the church was comprised of Palestinian Aramaic-speaking Jews. As the church spread into Gentile areas where the dominant language was Greek, the church was called upon to translate as well as interpret its traditions for an audience comprised of Greek-speaking Jews; in the Gentile territories, the church found a fruitful mission field among non-Jews. This new setting required that the originally Semitic traditions about Jesus be adapted for use in the Greek world. In other words, the Jesus traditions had to be "translated" for use in new social and cultural settings. It is not possible to translate without interpreting.

Another aspect of this form-critical model is that there are no assured channels of preservation. Anonymous Christians were the preservers and guarantors of the tradition, rather than (as in the traditional view) certain named apostles. Thus, the church preserved the tradition, and at the same time also created it. What was received by the gospel writers was a tradition that already bore the unmistakable imprint of those cultural stages and the anonymous persons that had used and passed on the tradition.[17]

The Call for an Oral Hermeneutic

A little over ten years ago Werner Kelber criticized form-critical scholars for not having a true "oral hermeneutic" to explain the circumstances of the Jesus traditions in the oral period prior to the writing of the gospels. By "oral hermeneutic" Kelber meant that principles for explaining the composition and transmission of the tradition should derive specifically from a study of orality. According to Kelber, the form critics were too influenced by literacy in developing their model to explain the oral period of the Jesus traditions. He points out that contemporary theorists are agreed that these two contexts (orality=spoken words and literacy =written words) are sufficiently different as to require a separate hermeneutic for each.

Kelber's features describing the composition and transmission of oral language as opposed to written language are worth reviewing:[18]

(1) In an oral context, a speaker addresses an audience whose presence influences both the shape and content of the address. An author of a written text, however, works in private for readers that are absent at the time of composition.

(2) The speaker, in order to assist memory, employs linguistic devices such as formulae and mnemonic patterns—techniques that an author of a written text would find unnecessary. The author, in contrast, working in the study, is free from the pressure of a live audience and the necessity of developing formulae and mnemonic devices to aid memory.

(3) Because the speaker is relying on memory and is influenced by the circumstances of delivery, it is axiomatic that not all available information gets told.

(4) The fate of all oral performers is the same: they risk being misunderstood and their words disappear the instant they are spoken. Hence it is unlikely that oral performers taught with a conscious concern that their words be reduced to writing. If they had such a concern, they would have been authors.

(5) Oral performers have something to say and seek out an audience for that reason. Some of what they said (if memorable) would have been remembered and passed on during their lifetime.[19]

(6) Nothing in the early Christian gospels suggests that the Jesus tradition was memorized by repetition and rote.

(7) Oral speech is socialized; that is to say, it reflects the characteristics of the social contexts in which it was performed. Hence a theory of oral transmission will involve detailed study of the social contexts of the oral period.

(8) Oral transmission is controlled by the law of "social identification." Social identification means that people will only remember that with which they can identify, whether positively or negatively.

(9) The fact that "distinct forms of speech can and do function in more than one social setting" challenges the idea of the form critics that "life setting" determines the distinctive form of material.

(10) Both the effectiveness and memorability of spoken words are enhanced or reduced in proportion to their conformity with rhythmic and acoustic concerns.

(11) The oral tradition is created and transmitted through individual performers. While the individual performers of the Jesus traditions will forever remain anonymous, "this is not the same thing as saying

that the Jesus traditions are rooted in the anonymous matrix of the community."

(12) If a tradition is alien to an audience, it will not be transmitted in that form, but will be adjusted to conform to social expectations or eliminated altogether. Kelber refers to this as "preventive censorship."

(13) The tendency of the oral tradition is to reduce the narrative unit to a memorable core, eliminating whatever is unnecessary to its essential character; that is to say, in an oral context the tradition tends to be abbreviated.

(14) In oral tradition "stock features are combined and reshuffled in endless variations, one theme is substituted for another, the order of sequences is changed, features are adopted from related or unrelated materials and variant compositions are forever in the making."

(15) There is no such thing as an "original form" in oral tradition. Each performance is a unique creation. Hence the form-critical search for an archetypal form reflects a textual orientation.

(16) In orality, tradition is almost always composition in transmission; it is not the passing on of established and fixed forms, but each new performance reshapes the narrative unit.

∞ THE EFFECTS OF THE ORAL PERIOD ON THE JESUS TRADITIONS[20]

If oral tradition works as Kelber and the form critics argue, what would have been its probable effect on the Jesus traditions?

A "Life of Jesus" and Oral Tradition

No connected account of Jesus' life was preserved in the oral tradition. This conclusion was also shared by Christians in the early second century—to judge from the report of Papias. The oral tradition tended to abbreviate and reduce individual sayings to an easily remembered core. This tendency makes it less likely that anything like a connected account of Jesus' life was ever preserved. A sequence connecting the major events of his life, his deeds, and public discourse with their original geographical and social contexts in which they occurred is not easily retained in memory. Nor was the church necessarily interested in preserving such historical memories given the impetus of its preaching about his resurrection. An outline of what the early church preached about Jesus (its "kerygma" = proclamation) is preserved, however, and it was easily remembered. Acts 2:22–24 sets out the scheme in its briefest form.[21] This brief outline mirrors the broader structure of Mark's gospel: "a man attested by God with mighty works, wonders, and signs" (=Mark 1–13) was "delivered up, crucified, and raised up" (=Mark 14–16). From this perspective Mark's gospel appears more as expanded kerygma than it does as conscious biography.

Little personal information about the life of Jesus would have been transmitted. In all likelihood, immediately after Easter people would be less motivated to pass on biographical details about the life of Jesus. In the faith of the church, Jesus was the resurrected Lord. What possible significance could biographical information have? What did he look like? Who were his friends? How did he spend his spare time? Where did he stay when he traveled away from home? What was his home life like? How tall was he? These questions were not germane to early Christian faith, and hence such information was never addressed in the oral tradition. Accordingly, the gospels preserved virtually nothing in the way of personal information about him.

Recollection and Christian Faith

Details were remembered because they were significant for faith. People simply do not, as a general rule, recall the specifics of events and details of conversations unless they have some reason for doing so, or unless something truly memorable occurred. The commonplace, the everyday, the banal, are rapidly forgotten—unless there is a significant reason for remembering it. That would have been true of the Jesus traditions as well. In Luke 14:8–10, for example, the reader is presented with a bit of advice on table etiquette at banquets; it is a bit of commonplace wisdom about how to comport oneself at a marriage feast. Luke calls the saying a "parable" (14:7), thus implying that it signifies more than it says. Luke even provides an interpretive conclusion to the saying, as has been provided for other parables (cf. Luke 18:14b); the interpretation takes the banal wisdom on table manners as a reference to the eschatological reversal that will come at the end of time (compare the material that follows the teaching on table etiquette, 14:12–24). Luke reported the advice on table manners not for what it said, but for what it was taken to mean.

Oral Transmission and Interpretation

Diverse interpretations were given to the same datum during oral transmission. If it is true that people remember things for reasons significant to each person, then the sayings of Jesus will be transmitted with various interpretations. Since people process language based on their particular circumstances of life, multiple "meanings" are inevitably bestowed on things Jesus said; hence different interpretations are the rule. The different interpretations to the same saying in the written gospels themselves is in many ways the legacy of their oral transmission. The parable of the Lost Sheep (Luke 15:1–7=Matt 18:10–14=*Gos Thom*, logion 107) is only one example. Matthew and Luke each place the parable in a different literary context. For Luke, Jesus spoke the parable in defense of his table fellowship with tax collectors and sinners (15:1–2), where, not surprisingly, the parable related to the salvation of sinners (15:7). In Matthew, the saying is included in a speech of Jesus to his disciples; thus, the interpretation of the parable appropriately relates to the security of the individual believer (Matt 18:14). The *Gospel of Thomas*, on the other hand, mentions no specific social setting, and does not append a formal interpretation, but this does not imply that the *Gospel of Thomas* had no understanding of the story. The noninterpretive ending is yet a third way the story was treated in antiquity. In the *Gospel of Thomas* readers were invited to look for "meanings" (*Gos Thom*, logion 1); hence they were not generally provided with specific "meanings." In the same way, sayings were given diverse interpretations during oral transmission.

During the oral period the distinction between the original tradition and its interpretation blurred. The example just given is a case in point. Matthew and Luke give the interpretation as a saying of Jesus himself. Perhaps the classic example of multiple interpretations for a single parable is Luke 16:1–13. The story proper appears in Luke 16:1–7. Luke 16:8–13 are various extraneous interpretations of the parable (8, 9, 10–12, 13) Luke received, either already associated with the parable or as individual sayings Luke found in the oral tradition (16:8–12) or Q (16:13) and appended to the story as interpretations.

The Jesus Tradition and Its Social Contexts

Jesus traditions were modified and adapted to suit various social contexts. In theory Jesus traditions could have been performed and transmitted in countless social contexts. Practically, however, the use of Jesus traditions would have been limited to the life of the church in the context of its preaching, teaching, debate, worship, and prophetic utterance. Where else, except among his followers, would it have been important to rehearse the sayings and deeds of Jesus? In each new social situation the tradition would have been modified to meet the religious needs of the church, as was seen in the case of Luke 15:1–7=Matt 18:10–14=*Gos Thom,* logion 107. While the original social settings for the sayings of Jesus are unknown, it is possible to see how the gospel writers derived different interpretations for sayings by adjusting their literary contexts. For example, on the one hand, placing Matt 7:2b ("The measure you give will be the measure you get") immediately after Matt 7:1–2a suggests that "you" will be "judged" by the same standards you use to judge others. On the other hand, precisely the same saying in Luke 6:38c ("The measure you give will be the measure you get back") under the influence of Luke 6:37–38b suggests that "you" will be "abundantly blessed" as you give to others.

Some sayings and stories used in the oral period may not have originated with Jesus. An early Christian listening to a sermon could easily confuse the speaker's memorable interpretation of a saying of Jesus as the voice of Jesus himself. The pronouncement of an early Christian prophet, prefaced by "thus says the Lord," could easily become a saying of Jesus. An unambiguous example of one saying that clearly did not originate with Jesus is Luke 4:23, "Physician, heal yourself." Luke portrays Jesus presenting it as a traditional proverb and not as something Jesus originally said. The general reader, however, tends to take it as a Jesus saying; nevertheless, it is a traditional proverb that appears in different versions elsewhere in the ancient world. It actually originated before the time of Jesus.[22] Hence Jesus could have repeated it, but he did not originate it.

Traditional sayings of Jesus tend to reflect linguistic features of the cultural environments in which they were performed or in which they originated. In the early period this involved at least two cultures, the Palestinian (Semitic) and Hellenistic (Greek). Jesus unquestionably spoke Aramaic.[23] While he and many of his listeners probably spoke Greek,[24] he would have addressed large groups in Aramaic, the native language of Jews in Palestine. Sometime between the Semitic world of Jesus and the composition of the gospels in Greek, Christians shifted their focus to the Hellenistic world where they preached to people whose culture and language were different from the language and culture of the original tradition. As a result, the Semitic tradition had to be adapted to the new Hellenistic environment. The adaptation involved in some cases substantive rather than cosmetic changes. For example, in Matt 5:18 (=Luke 16:17) Jesus affirms the abiding authority of the Jewish law: "Till heaven and earth pass away, not an iota, not a hook, will pass from the law until all is accomplished." An *iota* is the smallest letter in the Greek language; *hook* likely refers to tiny breathing marks (shaped like a hook) appearing over the initial vowels of Greek words or possibly a tiny iota subscript (shaped like a hook) that appears beneath certain Greek vowels. The saying in this form is geared to a Greek-speaking audience. Because of these linguistic features, Matt 5:18 is a saying likely created in a Greek-speaking language world after the time of Jesus, or a bit of original tradition transformed and adapted for a Greek-speaking audience.

If these conclusions are correct, it should dramatically affect how the early Christian gospels are read. For one thing, it is impossible to assume that sayings in the gospels are the exact words Jesus spoke. Additional implications include this problem: how can the voice of the historical man be distinguished from his many interpreters?

∞ ORAL TRADITION AND WRITTEN GOSPELS

On the one hand, the written gospels signal the beginning of the end of the oral process for stories and sayings reduced from living discourse to script, and embedded in a narrative. On the other hand, the gospels document a process of textual transmission involving a different set of principles.[25] Oral transmission of tradition did not end with the writing of the gospels, but continued as a competing source for the Jesus tradition. Even those stories and sayings trapped in the web of gospel narratives continued to circulate orally, subtly competing with their written counterparts. But the emergence of written texts altered the situation for the Jesus tradition, and reliance on the written words eventually replaced the use of the spoken words. Gospels composed in the middle to late first century will therefore likely reflect at least some features of their oral heritage.

A Limited Number of Literary Forms

A striking feature of gospel literature is its appearance of having been assembled out of a limited number of clearly identifiable smaller units of traditional material. In other words, the gospel writers collected pieces of the existing oral tradition to use in composing their gospels, but in the process they did not completely eradicate the formal patterns these traditions had assumed during their oral transmission. The assumption that such patterns existed in the oral period is explained in the following way. In the oral period, Jesus traditions were reduced by frequent repetition to a limited number of specific forms, easier to remember because of their formulaic character.

Although the form critics do not completely agree on terminology and types of literature, form-critical analysis has identified specific literary types in gospel literature: miracle stories, pronouncement stories, sayings, parables (i.e., brief fiction narratives), and stories about Jesus.[26] The presence of these forms argues strongly that the Jesus traditions were transmitted orally before being written down.

Vestiges of Early Oral Collections in the Written Gospels?

The presence of collections of these literary types in gospel literature suggests that oral material may have been received by the gospel writers as collections of similar types of material. The Sermon on the Mount (Matt 5–7), for example, is a collection of sayings,[27] and an early pre-Markan parables collection may well lie behind Mark 4.[28] The *Gospel of Thomas* and Q are simply sayings collections with little narrative framework. This is not to imply that the gospel writers were simply collectors who woodenly transmitted with no modification the traditional material they received. They were also "authors" and theologians who modified and adapted their material as they thought necessary to achieve their purposes.[29]

Orality and Textual Transmission

Chapter 5 noted that copyists sometimes harmonized the texts to correspond to other texts or to their own memory. Other changes crept into the written texts due to oral/aural slips.[30] It is always easy to mistake one word for another very similar word. A classic example of confusion from these "errors of the ear" occurs in Rom 5:1. Did Paul say, "we have (ἔχομεν) peace with God"? Or did he say, "let us have (ἔχωμεν) peace with God"? The one different Greek letter in each word (omicron/omega) makes them two different Greek verbal forms, which, although pronounced similarly, have two different meanings.

We have similar phenomena in English. Consider the following: pair/pear, deer/dear, peace/piece, bough/bow, base/bass, etc. Such word pairs are a breeding ground for mistakes of the ear in both the oral and even textual transmission of sayings, when someone is reading a text for others to copy. For example: If you say, "When John took the stage to perform, the entire crowd was amused by his feat." But your audience hears, "When John took the stage to perform, the entire crowd was amused by his feet," the difference in understanding is considerable. Yet both statements sound exactly the same.

∞

The recognition that the written gospels are comprised, at least in part, of traditional material that antedates their composition authorizes an investigation of the Jesus traditions in the oral period. Is it possible to distinguish earlier oral forms of the written tradition? Can some of those earlier oral forms be traced to the historical man, Jesus of Nazareth, with a degree of certainty higher than that accorded other forms? Some scholars answer those questions in the affirmative and have developed criteria for sorting out earlier forms of the tradition from later forms, as well as criteria for sorting out sayings that more probably originated with Jesus of Nazareth from sayings that less likely came from Jesus. These criteria for determining the originality of the Jesus tradition will be examined in the last chapter.

◌ RECOMMENDED READING AND SOURCES CONSULTED

BULTMANN, RUDOLF. *The History of the Synoptic Tradition.* Translated by John Marsh. Oxford: Blackwell, 1963. Reprint, Peabody, Mass.: Hendrickson, 1992. BYNUM, DAVID E. *The Daemon in the Wood: A Study of Oral Narrative Patterns.* Cambridge: Harvard University Press, 1978. CROSSAN, JOHN DOMINIC. *In Fragments: The Aphorisms of Jesus.* San Francisco: Harper & Row, 1983. DEWEY, JOANNA, ed. *Orality and Textuality in Early Christian Literature. Semeia* 65. Atlanta: Scholars Press, 1995. DIBELIUS, MARTIN. *From Tradition to Gospel.* 1935. Reprint, Greenwood, S.C.: Attic Press, 1971. DODD, C. H. *The Apostolic Preaching and Its Development.* London: Hodder & Stoughton, 1936. DUGGAN, J. J., ed. *Oral Literature. Seven Essays.* New York: Barnes & Noble, 1975. GERHARDSSON, BIRGER. *Memory and Manuscript.* 2d ed. Uppsala: C. W. K. Gleerup, 1964. GERHARDSSON, BIRGER. *The Origins of the Gospel Traditions.* Philadelphia: Fortress, 1979. KELBER, WERNER. *The Oral and the Written Gospel: The Hermeneutics of Speaking and Writing in the Synoptic Tradition, Mark, Paul, and Q.* Philadelphia: Fortress, 1983 (reprinted in 1997 with a new introduction). LORD, ALBERT B. *The Singer of Tales.* New York: Atheneum, 1978. NICKLE, KEITH F. *The Synoptic Gospels: An Introduction.* Atlanta: John Knox Press, 1980. ONG, WALTER J. *Orality and Literacy: The Technologizing of the Word.* London: Methuen, 1982. PARRY, MILMAN. *The Making of Homeric Verse: The Collected Papers of Milman Parry.* Edited by Adam Parry. Oxford: Oxford University Press, 1987. TAYLOR, VINCENT. *The Formation of the Gospel Tradition.* 2d ed. London: Macmillan, 1935. THOMAS, ROSALIND. *Literacy and Orality in Ancient Greece.* Cambridge: Cambridge University Press, 1992. Pages 29–51. TYSON, *New Testament and Early Christianity.* WATTS, ANN C. *The Lyre and the Harp: A Comparative Reconsideration of Oral Tradition in Homer and Old English Epic.* New Haven: Yale University Press, 1969.

◌ ISSUES FOR STUDY AND DISCUSSION

1. Read Matt 18:1–19:1. Is it a well-constructed speech with a single integrating theme that lends cohesion to the section? Does it appear to be more like an extraneous collection of sayings? How seriously should one consider Matthew's statement that these are (individual) "sayings" (19:1), rather than a single speech delivered on one particular occasion?

2. Read Matt 18:1–19:1 again. Identify sayings that can stand independently of the context and make reasonably good sense in isolation from the others.

3. Read Matt 18:1–19:1 again. Do you notice any organizing principle(s) to the sayings in the chapter? For example, verses 6, 7, and 8–9 appear to be three independent sayings connected by the same words (i.e., sin or stumble) "hooking" the extraneous sayings together. Are there other sayings in the chapter that appear to be "hooked" together in a similar way?

4. Read the following miracle stories and identify the main elements of their literary form: Mark 1:40–45; 1:29–31; 3:1–6; 4:35–41; 5:1–20. How are these miracle stories different?

5. Compare the following versions of the same parable: Matt 21:33–43, Mark 12:1–11, Luke 20:9–18, Gos Thom, logia 65–66. What constitutes the limits of the parabolic story in each version? Which version of the story is the most elaborate; which the simplest? Assume that these versions were oral and not written, and explain the elaboration and the abbreviation.

6. Make an experiment in the oral transmission of sayings with ten to fifteen people in the following way: Take one person out of the room and tell him or her a joke or a brief narrative you have written out (to show everyone later). The narrative is passed orally in succession from person to person outside the room. At the end compare the oral report to your written report. How do you explain the similarity and diversity? How does this experiment compare to the oral transmission of Jesus' sayings?

7. Compare Mark 9:40, Luke 9:50b, Matt 12:30, and Luke 11:23. Would you call these differences substantive or cosmetic and why? Would you consider them variations in an oral performance or deliberate scribal changes and why?

8. Identify and discuss the different cultural environments in antiquity in which the Jesus traditions were transmitted. Identify and discuss various social occasions where one might expect the Jesus tradition to have been performed. How do you suppose the various cultural environments, audiences, and social settings affected the shape and performance of the Jesus traditions?

9. In what ways was the first-century Hellenistic world different from the Semitic world of the same period?

10. How were the social circumstances of Jesus' ministry among Galilean peasants different from that of Paul's ministry among churches in the Hellenistic world?

8

EARLY CHRISTIAN PROPHETS AND THE JESUS TRADITION

The prophetic literature of the eighth and seventh centuries B.C.E. represents the flowering of prophecy in Israel, though the roots of prophecy in the Israelite tradition are much earlier (represented, for example, by such figures as Samuel, Elijah, and Elisha). Prophecy did not end with Israel's prophetic books of the seventh century, but continued into Second Temple Judaism.[1] Prophecy was not unique to the Israelites but was a cultural phenomenon throughout the ancient Near East and Greco-Roman world.[2] Israel's neighbors had prophets, as did the Greco-Roman religions.

In brief, and in general, a prophet served as a recognized and legitimate spokesperson for the deity through a variety of means.[3] Hence they were consulted or, on their own initiative, spoke for the deity. Their utterances are generally called "oracles," i.e., a divine message or saying.

In the Hellenistic world those who delivered such utterances were themselves called "oracles" as were the sites of the delivery of the oracles. People consulted oracles at numerous shrines throughout the ancient Hellenistic world. Two of the most famous were the oracles of Apollo at Delphi in Greece, and Didyma in Anatolia. At such centers people asked specific questions concerning their life, happiness, or fortune. The oracle's generally enigmatic response required interpretation or clarification. Early Christianity, in contrast, erected no shrines, and the prophetic voice could be spontaneous, being initiated by the deity, rather than by questions put to the prophet.[4]

During the early development of the Jesus tradition (roughly 30–70 C.E.), before the sayings of Jesus were incorporated into narrative gospels, prophets circulated among the early Christian communities (e.g., *Did.* 11:3–13:7). Spontaneously moved by the Spirit (Holy Spirit, Spirit of God, Spirit of Jesus), they spoke the "word of the Lord" to their contemporaries. Their prophecy was "immediately inspired." This means it was not a "reading" from a previously prepared script; rather it was regarded as God's instant utterance, the voice of the deity addressing a particular contemporary situation through the mouth of the prophet. While the early Christians thought all believers possessed the Spirit of God (Spirit of Jesus, Holy Spirit), they did not think all Christians were prophets (cf. 1 Cor 12:10, 29), but regarded the prophet as exercising a special function in the charismatic community.

∞ THE ISSUE: THUS SAITH THE LORD

Prior to the writing of the gospels, two kinds of sayings attributed to Jesus circulated in Christian oral tradition. On the one hand, the church remembered and passed on sayings of Jesus the historical man, such as Acts 20:35 and 1 Cor 11:23–25. These sayings, as was seen in an earlier chapter, were passed on by the church as something that Jesus had *previously* said that continued to be relevant to the church. On the other hand, sayings of early Christian prophets were offered as a *current* message from the resurrected Lord, who was now saying something new to the church. The former constituted reports of the Lord's *previous* address and the latter were presented as the Lord's *current* address to the church.

Any Christian in the context of preaching the gospel might report what the historical Jesus had previously said, but only through early Christian prophets could the continuing voice of the resurrected Lord be heard as direct address to the congregation. The early Christian prophet was not simply reporting what Jesus might have said had he been present. On the contrary, the prophet claimed to be speaking the very words of the Lord. The voice was the voice of the prophet, but the words were the words of the Lord.

The evolving oral tradition made no distinction between the prophetic word of the Lord and the word of the historical man. Sayings of Jesus uttered in the context of his public career prior to the crucifixion could be taken up by a later Christian prophet and applied to the new situation of the church as a new saying of the resurrected Lord. This is understandable, since the early Christians did not distinguish between the historical man and the risen Christ. The church regarded them both as one and the same, and hence both were designated by the titles "Christ" and "Lord."

Early Christians recognized no difference between what Jesus the historical man *said* during his public career in Palestine and what the resurrected Christ *continued to say* through early Christian prophets in the later communities.[5]

To many modern scholars, however, distinguishing between sayings of the historical man and sayings early Christian prophets spoke on behalf of the risen Christ seems crucial. For one reason, the social locations of such sayings differ. One set of sayings originated in the mind and life experience of Jesus the historical man, and the first time they ring in anyone's ears, they come from his lips. The other set of sayings originated in the mind and life experience of an early Christian prophet, and their first audition occurs in a social circumstance other than that experienced by Jesus as historical man. To be sure, early Christians *believed* that the resurrected Christ inspired the words, but even then the saying of the Lord was mediated through the mind and life experience of the prophet.[6]

Simply stated the issue is this: Have sayings of the resurrected Lord, originating in the mind and life experience of early Christian prophets, been included in the early Christian gospels as sayings of Jesus, the historical man? The early Christian tradition regarded them as genuine sayings of "the Lord," but their different historical and social locations clearly invalidate them as sayings of the historical man.

∞ PROPHETS IN THE EARLY CHURCH

This section considers the evidence for the activity of prophets in the early Christian communities, particularly prior to the writing of the gospels. Without question, prophets were active in the churches in the years preceding the writing of the gospels.[7] For example, evidence of early Christian prophets (1 Thess 5:19–21) can be found in the earliest extant Christian text (dated 50–51). The charismatic Pauline community at Corinth believed that prophets (1 Cor 12:10–11, 28) possessed a special gift of the Spirit (1 Cor 12:4–11, 28). Paul did not think that all Christians were prophets, at least not in the narrow sense that it has been defined in this chapter (1 Cor 12:29: the question "not all are prophets, are they?" expects a negative answer). There were both male and female prophets in the church (1 Cor 11:4–5). While the Corinthians thought of the prophetic experience as an involuntary possession of the Spirit, Paul disagreed and argued that the Spirit of the prophet could be controlled (1 Cor 14:26–33).

The author of the book of Acts, purportedly describing the early history of the church prior to 70 C.E.,[8] regards prophets as an established part of the early Christian landscape. Both male (Acts 11:27–28; 13:1; 15:32; 21:8–11) and female (Acts 21:8–9) prophets are found in the churches in Acts. Even Paul is regarded as a prophet, or portrayed functioning as a prophet; at least he is described in situations where the resurrected Lord speaks to him (Acts 9:3–6; 16:6–7; 18:9–10; 20:22–23; 22:7–10). In Acts, early Christian prophets are portrayed proclaiming new sayings of the resurrected Lord as current address (11:28; 13:2; 21:10–11; 23:11; cf. 27:23–24).

Even in his letters Paul appears to fit the description of an early Christian prophet.

> He is an immediately inspired spokesman for the risen Lord, who receives revelations that he is impelled to deliver to the Christian community (cf., e.g., 1 Cor. 2:13; 5:3–4; 7:40; 14:6, 37; 2 Cor. 2:17; 12:1–9, 19; 13:3; Gal. 1:12; 2:2; 1 Thess. 2:13; 4:1–2, 15–17).[9]

For a clear instance of Paul's repeating a word from the resurrected Lord see 2 Cor 12:9;[10] many scholars also regard 1 Cor 15:51–52 as another word of the resurrected Lord to Paul.[11]

∞ THE EARLY CHRISTIAN PROPHETIC IMAGINATION

The gospels of Matthew, Luke, and John portray the followers of Jesus as receiving new revelations from the resurrected Lord (Matt 28:9–20; Luke 24; John 20–21). Twice, the women followers of Jesus appear to function as prophets, presenting "new" sayings of Jesus to the male disciples (Luke 24:9–11; John 20:18; but Matt 28:9–11 appears to be a word of the resurrected Lord that the women did not deliver: to Matt 28:16 compare 26:32 and Mark 16:8).[12] While the reporting of these situations is later than the writing of Mark's gospel (around 70), they do afford insight into how the church imagined the new revelations happened. With the exception of certain passages in Paul (Gal 1:12; 2:2; 1 Cor 14:6; 2 Cor 12:1–10; 13:3), the gospels provide the earliest written descriptions of how the first-century church conceived of prophets receiving their messages from the resurrected Lord.

The inspiration of the prophet is generally conceived to occur in the context of visions. In 2 Cor 12:1–3, 7, Paul describes his revelations from the Lord (2 Cor 12:7) as if they had occurred in a vision (2 Cor 12:1–3). Visions and dreams appear to be the dominant way revelations were conceived as being transmitted in Acts (9:3–6, 10–17; 10:9–21, 30–33; 11:4–12; 16:6–10; 18:9–10; 22:6–11; 26:12–18; 27:23–26).

In the Apocalypse (the book of Revelation) John describes himself as a "brother to the seven churches [of Asia]" (1:9). The narrator of the first prologue (1:1–3) describes him as a "servant" (1:1), but an angel at the conclusion of the book numbers him among "the prophets" (22:9), and his "book" is regarded as a prophecy (1:1–3; 22:7, 10, 18–19). More significantly, John functions as a prophet. While he is "in the spirit on the Lord's day," he hears behind him a voice telling him to write what he sees in a book and send it to the seven churches of Asia (1:10–11).[13] What follows that directive is a rather grotesque description (1:12–16) of the resurrected Lord, the only detailed description in early Christian literature. This figure directs John to write specific messages to the angels of the seven churches (1:17–20).

The messages to the "angels" (2:1–3:22) constitute the words of the resurrected Lord. John presents them as new sayings from the Lord rather than remembered sayings of something the Lord had said earlier. They come to the prophet in the context of a vision (like similar reports in Acts) originating in the context of John's faith and life situation. The words are created *de novo* as direct personal address to the seven churches in Asia. The first time these particular words are "heard" or "seen" is through the mouth, or pen, of the prophet John. It is always possible, of course, that some of these "new" sayings were actually older traditional sayings of Jesus that were reused by the prophet in this context, but that would have to be demonstrated.[14] In any case they are not presented as sayings of Jesus the historical man, but rather as sayings of the resurrected Christ.

∞ ARE THERE ORACLES OF THE RESURRECTED LORD IN THE GOSPELS?[15]

Some scholars detect oracles of the resurrected Lord in the gospels. These are sayings of early Christian prophets spoken in the period 30–70 that were caught up in the oral tradition. Later they came to be included in the canonical gospels as sayings of Jesus the historical man. M. E. Boring argues that fifteen sayings in Q probably originated as sayings of early Christian prophets: 6:22–23; 10:3, 4, 5–12, 13–15, 16, 21–22; 11:29b–30, 39–42; 12:8–9, 10, 11–12; 13:34–35; 16:17; 22:28–30.[16]

Boring identifies five passages in Mark as sayings of early Christian prophets: 3:28–29; 6:8–11; 8:38; 9:1; 13:5–31 (and possibly 10:45);[17] he finds four in Matthew: 5:3–12; 5:18; 10:23; 28:18b–20.[18] Only one saying in Luke is unambiguously an early Christian oracle, 10:19–20.[19] All three gospels have other sayings that have been reworked by early Christian prophets.

Boring uses three criteria to identify sayings of the prophets in the gospels:[20] (a) the sayings must be able to make sense in and of themselves without relying upon their literary context; (b) the sayings must be considered products of the church for reasons other than their similarity to Christian prophecy. This is because Jesus himself is portrayed as a charismatic and prophetic figure in the gospels, and hence his discourse may reflect characteristics of prophetic utterance. Then (c) Boring examines the sayings he has identified as prophetic to see if they reflect the characteristics of early Christian prophetic speech, as he reconstructed it.[21]

Mark 9:1 exemplifies Boring's rationale for identifying sayings of early Christian prophets. Mark 9:1 has an independent character, since it carries its own formulaic introduction and has no essential connection with its immediate narrative context. Mark 8:34–38 is a short speech of Jesus introduced with "and he called to him the multitude with his disciples and said to them." If 9:1 is a part of this short speech, as the context suggests, why does the author provide the saying in 9:1 with another introductory formula, "and he said to them"? This new and unnecessary introductory statement sets the saying off from the previous speech as an independent saying. The saying does not fit with what precedes or follows, hence it is unlikely that Mark created it; rather, it is better seen as a traditional saying that Mark appropriated from the oral tradition.

Mark 9:1 seems to reflect the later social environment of the postresurrection church, which anxiously awaited the absent Lord's return. The saying offers an encouraging word to the church, where some probably have already died (note that only *some* of those present will be alive to see the parousia). The situation reflected in the saying certainly does not reflect Jesus' situation around 30 C.E., since he is still present with the disciples. Boring argues that the saying clearly reflects the features of prophetic speech:

> the eschatological certainty of the coming of the Lord, the authority to make a declaration about its date, the introductory formula, "truly, truly I say to you," [the role of the saying in upbuilding, encouraging, and consoling the community], the similarity in form and function to 1 Cor. 15:51 and 1 Thess. 4:15–17 (prophetic oracles that speak to the same problem in the same way) and the formal similarity to Matt. 10:23. . . ."[22]

⚹

Clearly, early Christian prophets influenced the Jesus tradition in at least two ways: (a) they introduced new sayings of Jesus into the stream of oral tradition and (b) they revised other traditional sayings in line with their prophetic spirit.[23] Some of these created and revised sayings have been imported into the early Christian gospels, which purport to describe the public career of Jesus as "historical" man. The only question is how many can be found in the gospels. Scholars disagree on the extent of influence and on their ability to identify sayings that have been created or reformulated as prophetic sayings.[24] But the probability that such sayings do exist in the gospels raises the difficult issue of which sayings may be attributed to Jesus the historical man, which sayings may be assigned to the early church, and what are the criteria on which such decisions may be made. Not to consider the issue at all raises the problem of the credibility of the portraits of Jesus presented in the gospels. How closely do those portraits approximate the historical figure? To put the matter a bit differently: can the historical man, Jesus of Nazareth, bear the weight of the very generous interpretations of him presented by the early Christian evangelists? To some extent that may be a question faith decides, but it is at the very least partially a question for the historian.

∞ RECOMMENDED READING AND SOURCES CONSULTED

AUNE, D. E. *Prophecy in Early Christianity.* Grand Rapids: Eerdmans, 1983. BORING, M. E. *The Continuing Voice of Jesus: Christian Prophecy and the Gospel Tradition.* Louisville: Westminster John Knox, 1991. BORING, M. E. *Sayings of the Risen Jesus: Christian Prophecy in the Synoptic Tradition.* SNTSMS 46. Cambridge: Cambridge University Press, 1982. GILLESPIE, T. W. *The First Theologians: A Study in Christian Prophecy.* Grand Rapids: Eerdmans, 1994.

∞ ISSUES FOR STUDY AND DISCUSSION

1. Read Boring, Continuing Voice of Jesus, *155–86 and list Boring's principal characteristics of prophetic speech.*

2. Is 2 Cor 12:9 a saying of Jesus the historical man or a saying of the resurrected Lord? Explain your reasons.

3. Select two of the following sayings and discuss why they might be considered sayings of an early Christian prophet, or a saying reformulated by a prophet:

Q 6:20b–21	Matt 13:35
Q 10:2	Matt 17:20
Matt 5:19	Luke 10:18
Matt 7:2	Luke 12:32

4. Select one of the passages below and discuss whether or not it should be re-garded as a saying of an early Christian prophet: Rev 1:7–8; 3:20; 16:15; 19:9; 22:7a, 12–14.

5. Select two of the following and list the evidence for early Christian prophecy in them:

Colossians	the Pastoral Epistles (1–2 Timothy, Titus)
Ephesians	1–2 Peter
Hebrews	2 Thessalonians
James	

6. Are the sayings of the resurrected Lord in Matt 28 and Luke 24 sayings of early Christian prophets, nonprophetic creations of the evangelists, or traditional sayings of the historical man? Are there other options? How would one determine the original social setting of the sayings?

9

SEARCHING FOR JESUS AMONG THE CHRISTS OF EARLY CHRISTIAN FAITHS

The prospects of reconstructing a reliable, widely accepted, historical account of the public career of Jesus are not promising. Given the nature of the materials, even reconstructing a simple historical sequence for his public career is not possible—at least not a sequence that could accommodate all the sources, survive a rigorous historical critique, and satisfy a majority of historians. The variation in the sequences of events between John's gospel and the synoptic gospels, and among the synoptics themselves, mandates that one sequence be chosen from among the four, or that all four be harmonized. These two solutions appear arbitrary at best.

Further, the character of Jesus is remarkably different in each gospel. Each writer derived different impressions of Jesus from the available oral and written traditions, and subsequently they shaped their portraits in line with a particular theological understanding. Under these conditions the possibility of determining which impression actually captures the essence of the historical man seems slight. Since "impressions" are subjective, all five gospels are possibly either "correct" to some degree or completely wide of the mark. No disinterested, objective standard exists for measuring their impressions. Further, the oral and written traditions, from which the evangelists developed their particular portraits, were themselves shaped in transmission. Reliable historical impressions of the man may be preserved in the gospels to some degree, but they are still nevertheless impressions and communicate only what others *thought* about him. Impressions are not hard historical data, but rather anecdotal information that helps the historian understand how Jesus' later admirers viewed him; we have no contemporary reports.

But Jesus' sayings are regarded as primary sources of information for the historical figure, even though they were molded and shaped in the process of transmission. The challenge lies in determining the extent of early Christian shaping of the sayings and eliminating sayings not originating with Jesus but which were caught up in the stream of early Christian tradition. Can sayings more probably originating with Jesus of Nazareth be distinguished from sayings less likely originating with him? Because the gospels (and the oral Jesus traditions) have been markedly shaped by early Christian faith, some way will have to be found to identify the later shaping by the church from those traditions that likely originated with Jesus.

∞ TERMINOLOGY AND DISCLAIMERS

Notice how the language in the introduction to this chapter has been stated: "more probably originating with Jesus"—"less likely originating." In other words, sorting out the sayings of a "historical Jesus" from the "Christs of early Christian faiths" is not an exact science. Evaluating sayings is better conceived as art, even though the assessment operates on the basis of scientific and historical principles. The result will not be an exact historical description of Jesus "as he actually was." Given the nature of the material, such a judgment is hardly possible. In fact, even in the first century an exact description of Jesus "as he actually was" would not have been possible. If three first-century historians who knew Jesus personally in his lifetime had decided to write an account of his public career, the accounts would have differed in various ways, just as modern biographies differ. Biographies are author's interpretations, and interpretations differ. Historically developed biographies will agree on the objective data of an individual's life, provided the data are matters of public record, but differences should be expected in how the data and the individual are assessed—just as we find in the early Christian gospel literature.

∞ WHERE TO BEGIN?

Two key assumptions underlie an attempt to recover the historical Jesus. (1) *Early Christian Gospel literature includes historical information about Jesus.* The foregoing pages have contended that the gospels in their diversity cannot possibly all be correct in everything they tell us about Jesus. The sheer diversity in their descriptions of him precludes this. But that is not the same as saying nothing in the gospels is historical. Hence the attempt to recover the historical Jesus positively assumes we can identify aspects of the life of the historical man from the gospels with some degree of certainty. (2) *Reconstructing historical aspects of Jesus' life is worth doing and to some extent possible.* What is the value of being able to say that a saying of Jesus or an aspect of his public career more probably derives from the historical man? The answer depends on why an individual is interested in Jesus. Some persons of religious faith confronted with the widespread diversity in the gospels might throw up their hands and say, "What's the use; how can you trust any of it?" These individuals can at least be assured that aspects of Jesus' life are grounded in history and not solely in the faith of the church.

Likewise historians need to recover historical aspects of Jesus' life. The historical evidence outside the New Testament does confirm his existence as a figure of human history, but it says nothing about the character of the man. Both the historian and the person of faith are concerned (but for different reasons) with the question: can the character of the historical man bear the weight of the interpretations of him provided in the early

Christian gospels? Put another way: What is the relationship between the historical man and the Christ of early Christian faiths? If there is no correlation, no history can be written, and the basis of Christianity could well dissolve into mythical narrative—stories about a god. Thus the following twin questions raise both historical and religious issues: Is there continuity between the Christ of faith and the historical man? How much continuity actually exists?

∞ CRITERIA USED TO DETERMINE THE ORIGINALITY OF JESUS' SAYINGS

Evaluating the sayings of Jesus as to originality is not a novelty of recent scholarship. The widening gap between Jesus the historical man and the Christ of early Christian faiths emerged in the eighteenth century during the Enlightenment.[1] Critical scholarship has ever since been forced to address the issue, as Albert Schweitzer's *Quest of the Historical Jesus* clearly shows. The problems raised by Schweitzer's book have not been resolved, and the gap between the historical man and the Christ of faith continues to enlarge.[2]

This section focuses on only four of the criteria currently used to validate sayings as more likely originating with Jesus. Norman Perrin popularized three of these criteria in his book *Rediscovering the Teaching of Jesus* (38–49).

Five general assumptions underlie this kind of analysis of the Jesus tradition. (1) *Jesus was a human being who lived during the early Roman Empire.* Like everyone else his life and character were shaped and molded by the culture around him. Thus his personal history may be investigated in the same way as any other person of his time. (2) *Jesus was a Jewish lad growing up in the first quarter of the first century C.E. in Galilee, a region of the early Roman province of Palestine.* His history and character development should be consistent with the Palestinian Judaism of that period. Features in accounts about him that are inconsistent with that cultural context must be regarded with skepticism. In particular, features suggesting Greek influence are suspect, since the latest phase of the early Christian movement was Gentile Greek Christianity, the phase producing the early Christian gospels. (3) *Jesus did not establish a reli-*

gious community. As Jews, the lives of the earliest followers and associates of Jesus accorded with the religious community of Palestinian Judaism. Jesus stood within Palestinian Judaism and critiqued it from the inside. Modeled on the synagogue and growing out of the subsequent Christian movement, the Christian church developed later. Thus, Jesus' sayings reflecting the features of in-group/out-group mentality derive from the later Christian movement claiming him as its founder. (4) *We can never investigate the history of Jesus directly.* He wrote nothing, and what is attributed to him was filtered through the religious experiences of his later followers in the Mediterranean basin for more than a quarter century. Thus we may hope to identify with the greatest confidence only the most distinctive features of his teaching: what is Jewish, but yet stands in tension with Palestinian Judaism; what is Christian, but yet stands in tension with the later Christian movement. (5) *The orthodox view of Jesus is not privileged in the investigation.* In fact, no particular ancient or contemporary view of Jesus is used as a standard by which sayings are evaluated. A historical profile of Jesus is developed from those sayings and traditions having the highest claim to originality, irrespective of its consistency or inconsistency with the later views of Christian orthodoxy.

The Criterion of Dissimilarity (or Distinctiveness)

Sayings and parables may be regarded as
original with Jesus if they are dissimilar to
characteristic emphases in Palestinian
Judaism and early Christianity.

This criterion, stated in a positive way, actually functions negatively. The vigorous demand of the criterion excludes from consideration the deeds of Jesus.[3] It even limits the scope of what he said to brief sentences (i.e., sayings) and stories Jesus told (i.e., parables). For example, the entire collection of discourses by Jesus in the Gospel of John (cf. ch. 15 or 17) are excluded, although individual sayings from these discourses may be considered.[4]

Behind this limitation lies the theory that the oral tradition did not transmit complete speeches.

The criterion of dissimilarity furthermore excludes all sayings and parables containing features similar to *characteristic* emphases in both Judaism and Christianity. For example, on the basis of this criterion the three passion–resurrection predictions of Jesus in the Gospel of Mark (8:31; 9:31; 10:32–34) must be excluded, because belief in Jesus' resurrection is a central feature of early Christian preaching and teaching. According to the criterion's logic, early Christians created the passion predictions and attributed them to Jesus to show that the death of Jesus was not accidental but rather a part of God's grand design (cf. Acts 2:23). Jesus knew beforehand that he would die and be raised. Hence God had planned for the cross all along. This rationale turned an obvious threat to faith into a strong reassurance.

The saying of Jesus on the permanence of the Jewish law (Matt 5:18) is excluded for the same reason. The Torah was a central feature of first-century Jewish teaching, and the earliest Christians were Jews. Certain early Christian groups continued teaching that the Torah was binding upon Christians (e.g., the opponents against whom Paul argued in Galatians), and they would want to show that the Torah was grounded in the teaching of Jesus. Hence the criterion of dissimilarity disqualifies Matt 5:18 as a saying of Jesus because it could be an early Christian creation to validate a central aspect of the faith.

It is entirely possible, however, that Jesus did predict his death and resurrection and also insisted the Torah was binding on his followers. But, it is equally plausible that both sayings were the products of early Christian piety.[5] They are eliminated, therefore, not because the argument disproves their origin with Jesus but because their origin in the early Christian movement cannot be disproved. In other words, one origin is as plausible as the other. And because the scholar is trying to identify sayings having a higher probability of originating with Jesus, those sayings only possibly made by Jesus are eliminated.

Matthew 5:44a ("love your enemies") is an example of a saying that probably did originate with the historical Jesus. The naked absolute "love your enemies" contrasts with Torah, which required the Hebrew people to "love their neighbors" (Lev 19:17–18, 33–34). And it also contrasts well with early Christians who, uncomfortable with the absolute, sought to qualify the saying in terms of specific acts that would be easier to do. Matthew (5:44b) qualifies "love your enemies" as meaning "pray for those who persecute you." Praying for your persecutors without actually loving them is a way around the absolute requirement to love them. The naked absolute "love your enemies," however, is actually a paradox: whoever loves their enemies has no enemies! Hence this saying starkly contrasts with Judaism and early Christianity and has no parallels in the ancient world. Most probably the command "love your enemies" is a saying of the historical man Jesus of Nazareth. Its origin with Jesus is more plausible than its origin with first-century Judaism and early Christianity.

The Criterion of Multiple Attestation

When a motif or a teaching attributed to Jesus appears in more than one literary form and more than one independent literary source, the possibility of its originality is increased, provided it is not characteristic of the early church or Palestinian Judaism.

This criterion does not validate individual sayings; rather, it affirms emphases or ideas. It looks for similar ideas expressed in different literary forms (i.e., aphorism, parable, etc.) and independent literary units of early Christian literature. The independent literary units are: Mark (assuming Mark is the earliest written gospel, Matthew and Luke are dependent on Mark), the *Gospel of Thomas*, Q, M (Matthew's special source), L (Luke's special source), John, and the letters of Paul. In both form and function, this criterion proceeds positively.

Behind the criterion of multiple attestation lies the following theory: when two or more independent sources preserve a similar teaching or idea, it is more plausible to assume that the ideas did not originate with the authors of the written texts, but rather antedated them. Hence similar ideas in different literary forms and in independent sources more likely are "traditional," i.e., the ideas are earlier than the texts in which they appear.[6]

Applying this criterion to the saying about "the prophet without honor" underscores the likelihood of its being a traditional saying that may have originated with Jesus. The saying appears in the independent sources Mark, John, and the *Gospel of Thomas:*

> A prophet is not without honor, except in his own country, and among his own kin, and in his own house (Mark 6:4).

> For Jesus himself testified that a prophet has no honor in his own country (John 4:44).

> A prophet is not acceptable in the prophet's own town (*Gos Thom* 31:1).

Note that the motif is found in three independent sources and in two different literary forms. Two are sayings attributed to Jesus (Mark and *Gospel of Thomas*) and the third is an early Christian report on something that Jesus reputedly said (John). Although the wording is different, an oral tradition attributing such an idea to Jesus must have existed prior to the writing of the texts.

Another similar example appears in the same sources.

> Destroy this temple and in three days I will raise it up (John 2:19).

> Aha! You who would destroy the temple and build it in three days, save yourself and come down from the cross (Mark 15:29; cf. Matt 26:61, 27:40).

> I shall destroy this house and no one will be able to build it [. . .] (*Gos Thom* 71).

Again the motif appears in two forms. Two of the sources report it as a saying of Jesus (John and *Gospel of Thomas*). The third saying appears on the lips of Jesus' accusers, as something he reputedly said (Mark). That some kind of saying about the destruction of the temple existed in the oral tradition appears more probable than reasoning that each author independently created such an idea. The criterion of multiple attestation only identifies motifs as traditional, however. Making a plausible case for originality requires a further argument. The idea's distinctiveness from the early church and first-century Judaism would need to be shown.

The Criterion of Coherence

Material from the earliest stratum of the Jesus tra-
dition may be original, provided it coheres with ma-
terial established as original by means of the
criterion of dissimilarity.

The term *material* incorporates both sayings and ideas. The requirement that the material come from the earliest stratum of the tradition means it must be identified as a traditional feature or saying, which existed as oral tradition prior to the writing of the text; thus, there is good reason to think it did not originate with the evangelist. The criterion of coherence is used most effectively in dealing with noncanonical texts by identifying material that closely coheres with (i.e., is similar to) material already established as original on the basis of the criterion of dissimilarity.

For example, critical scholars are quite optimistic that many of the parables in gospel literature originated with Jesus of Nazareth.[7] On the basis of this criterion, some scholars have argued for the originality of certain new parables of Jesus found in the *Gospel of Thomas* and the *Apocryphon of James*. One of those parables in the *Gospel of Thomas*, the Assassin (*Gos Thom* 98), has not yet been extensively studied, but scholars still tend to favor its originality.[8] The story with its questionable "hero" does recall those canonical parables where the story's hero also has a questionable character, such as the Unmerciful Servant (Matt 18:23–34) and the Unjust Steward (Luke 16:1–7). Some scholars see the slaying of the "powerful man" by the assassin, whom they take to be a "little guy," as a reversal theme, a feature associated with the parables originating with Jesus. The reversal theme appears in other stories of Jesus, such as the Pharisee and the Tax Collector, the Prodigal Son, and the Lost Sheep. Hence the story coheres with other stories thought to originate with Jesus on other grounds.

The violence reflected in the Assassin may well be the reason that it was not used by the canonical evangelists. They did have difficulty with stories that seemed to endorse antisocial behavior, as attested by the string of early Christian interpretations (Luke 16:8–13) appended to the Unjust Steward (Luke 16:1–7). That later

Christians would have invented such a violent story and attributed it to Jesus seems unlikely. Hence, on the basis of the criterion of coherence, in all likelihood the Assassin originated with the historical Jesus.

The Criterion of Linguistic and Environmental Tests

Material is to be rejected as original with Jesus if it is incompatible with the languages and social/cultural environment of first-century Palestine.

In this form the criterion is clearly negative; it can, however, be stated affirmatively:

Sayings that have the highest claim to originality are sayings that reflect an Aramaic language-world and the cultural context of first-century Palestinian Judaism.

Behind this criterion lies the theory that the historical Jesus was a product of his environment. He may in many ways have contrasted with his first-century world, but language that originated with him in the first century would inevitably have been compatible with the culture and environment that "produced" him.

The Jesus tradition is extant only in Greek. It is not preserved in Aramaic, the language of rural Palestine. Thus our sources for Jesus are one language-world removed from the vernacular of Jesus' world, since the gospels were written for a readership familiar with Greek. In other words, everything we have from and about Jesus was produced for the Hellenistic (i.e., Greek-speaking) church. Anything in the New Testament original with Jesus is already a translation and interpretation for people who lived later in a different cultural environment.

In many instances, however, scholars can show that numerous sayings still reflect aspects of the Palestinian world that nourished the historical Jesus (e.g., the parable of the Pharisee and Tax Collector, Luke 18:10–14a). In some cases, vestiges of Jesus' mother tongue, Aramaic, can be identified among the sayings attributed to him. For example, Luke 12:22–23 reflects a Hebrew poetic form, called synonymous parallelism, whereby the second line of a couplet expresses the same idea as the first line using different words.

> Do not be anxious about your life, what you shall eat,
>> nor about your body, what you shall wear.
> For life is more than food,
>> and the body more than clothing.

On the other hand, some sayings reflect a Hellenistic environment. In the discussion of the criterion of dissimilarity above, Matt 5:18 was judged less probably original with Jesus because it reflected a characteristic emphasis of Palestinian Judaism and Jewish Christianity. The criterion of linguistic and environmental tests provides another reason for rejecting this saying as an original utterance of Jesus. In its present form, the saying is conceptualized in Greek:

> Till heaven and earth pass away, not an *iota*, not a *hook*, will pass from the law till all is accomplished.

As noted earlier, the *iota* is the smallest of the Greek letters, and *hook* likely refers to a mark over initial vowels of Greek words. In its present form the saying would have meant little to an Aramaic-speaking audience, since the image would have made sense only to people who knew Greek. Hence in this form the saying is incompatible with the languages and environment of the public career of Jesus and therefore less likely originated with Jesus.[9]

Criticisms of the Criteria

Three main criticisms have been leveled against the use of these criteria.[10]

First, the Jesus recovered through the use of these criteria is not the historical man, but rather the historical man at his most radical dimensions. The criterion of dissimilarity eliminates what the Jesus of the evangelists has in common with characteristic emphases of Judaism and early Christianity, because the origin of the feature cannot be determined with certainty. But why would it be assumed that early Christians invented their central theological emphases rather than deriving them from Jesus? Isn't the simplest solution to assume they came from Jesus himself? And why wouldn't

Jesus as a Jew, have something in common with the characteristic values of Judaism? The dissimilarity criterion, however, has obliged the elimination of this material because neither source, Judaism/early Christianity or Jesus, can be given precedence over the other with a higher degree of probability. In short, one origin is as plausible as the other. Without this criterion, however, there is no way to distinguish Jesus from early Christian faith about him with a convincing higher degree of probability argument, and thus the historical man disappears, swallowed up in early Christian faith. Neither the church's Christ nor the scholars' historical Jesus will correlate exactly with the historical man of the first century.

Second, the criteria assume that scholarship fully understands the character of first-century Palestinian Judaism—which is true to some degree. But the truth of the situation is that while a great deal about the character of Palestinian life in the first century is known, much is not. Historians comprehend the ancient world of Jesus only in a general way. Each new discovery, however, improves knowledge and corrects the earlier consensus. This is not a criticism of the criteria, however, but rather an acknowledgment that what is brought to the table using the criteria is incomplete. That does not mean results are invalid, but only that results are tentative. Reaching conclusions in New Testament scholarship is a process whereby conclusions change with new information and arguments.

The third criticism, that new criteria will be developed in the future, is justified. And this has indeed already happened.[11] Yet new criteria will not render the current ones obsolete or invalidate their results. The new will come to supplement and correct the old. The rationale whereby the old criteria proceed will likely not be overturned.

New criteria may make it possible to add sayings to our current database of sayings judged original with Jesus. It is not likely that new criteria will further reduce the current critical database of sayings. It is difficult to conceive of a criterion stricter than the criterion of dissimilarity.

ꙮ Postscript: Science and Faith

Scholars evaluating the Jesus tradition by these and other historical criteria judge their own results with varying degrees of confidence. Some, more optimistically, regard their arguments as conclusively demonstrating a saying's originality or, conversely, showing that it could not be from the historical Jesus. Others are more cautious. They use the criteria but claim less certainty for their results. For the latter, results are always couched in terms of possibilities, probabilities, and improbabilities—not impossibilities and certainties.

The more conservative approach seems best. Everything attributed to Jesus in the ancient literature, both canonical and noncanonical, might *possibly* have been said by Jesus. But however well meaning, such a judgment is scarcely *probable*. Sayings that can pass rigorous historical criteria may be elevated on the basis of a convincing argument from possible to probable status. If a saying cannot be raised to a higher level of certainty (i.e., probable), it should remain only possible or, on the basis of a convincing argument against its originality, be downgraded to improbable (a lesser degree of certainty than possible). Nevertheless, improbable does not mean impossible; nor does probable mean certain. Although a saying is currently regarded as less probably a saying of Jesus, with the right argument it may in the future yet be raised to a higher level of certainty, i.e., possible or probable. As new criteria are developed and new information about Palestine in the first century becomes available, sayings formally judged only possible, or even improbable, under current criteria can be reevaluated and their categories changed.

Reconstructing any ancient figure requires the use of objective criteria to evaluate both sources and traditions. Not all sources or traditions have equal weight in the historian's reconstruction of the past, nor should they. Evaluating the relative reliability of the raw data is the first responsibility of the historian, for any history based on the improbable or the merely possible by definition is unreliable and misleading. The same holds true for historical reconstructions of the public career of Jesus. On the one hand, not to sift every available early source using rigorous historical criteria skews the reconstruction of Jesus in the direction of canonical faith. The application of rigorous historical criteria on every available early source, on the other hand, skews the reconstruction in the direction of a historical construct.

As a historical figure, Jesus is not above history; rather, he is a part of history and hence a fit subject for historical investigation. Historians should be as rigorous in studying Jesus of Nazareth as they are in studying any ancient historical figure. Not to do so seems to regard Jesus' own history as somehow less important than what one branch of early Christianity thought about him— i.e., to favor one religious interpretation over historical analysis of all data. To make such a judgment without first critically sifting the tradition (all of it) in terms of its historical reliability ensures the subordination of history to faith.

Is it possible to do both—to have faith in Jesus, and at the same time to study Jesus from a historian's perspective, or is the collision between history and faith so destructive that one approach must inevitably yield to the other? My answer to the first question is: "I think so"; to the second: "absolutely not." For me, it is more helpful to think of the canons of historical criticism and the demands of faith as terminal points at either end of a continuum from which I view the world, rather than as opposing philosophies. At the extremes, of course, one will always yield to the other, but along the continuum between the points they complement one another. For example, faith cannot demand I believe something that historical analysis can demonstrate to me to be patently false. At this point, faith must yield every time! On the other hand, mysteries in the universe remain that have not fallen before the assault of critical analysis. For example, medical science can manipulate the border between life and death by mechanically controlling the bodily processes necessary to organic existence. They use life support systems to do for the body what the body cannot do for itself. Thus, an inert comatose body can be provided breath, water, and nourishment. Yet medical science cannot restore quality life to someone when the brain, the organ controlling the body, ceases to function. Thus "life" itself remains a mystery, and tantalizingly out of the scientist's reach. Historians are in no position to demand that faith abandon the field to historical and scientific methodology because, undeniably, areas of human existence fall outside the domains of the scientist and the historian. History itself is not a completely consistent discipline. Historians using the same methodology can arrive at different conclusions. Thus, his-

torians may not legitimately demand that faith submit to historical methodology and ground itself in a historian's reconstruction
of Jesus, for not even the historians agree on how Jesus should be
understood.

For many, a way out of this seeming impasse between the demands of faith and history is found by situating themselves on the
continuum somewhere between the two extremes. No single point
on the continuum, however, offers a vantage that resolves all the
tensions between faith and history. Along the continuum between
the two extremes there will always be tension, not only because
new information continually becomes available and methodolo-
gies change, but also because individuals change. What satisfied
us at one stage of our intellectual development and religious odyssey may no longer satisfy us at another stage. And so we shift positions on the continuum moving more closely to one extreme or the
other, but the tension should always remain. Reducing the tension increases the risk that faith in Jesus may be abandoned, or, on
the other hand, that he will be dehistoricized. In this latter instance, the Jesus of faith is ruled exempt from historical analysis,
and thus Jesus' "history" slips into mythology, i.e., stories about a
god, whose personal history and world were not part of our own
common space and time.

Some Christians in the second century, and later, did exactly
that. Their dehistoricizing of Jesus led them to see him as non-
human. To be sure, he may have looked like us, but he was not one
of us. In their faith, he was completely a heavenly figure, whose
being was something other than human.

> ". . . he appeared on earth as a man and performed miracles . . . he
> did not suffer, but a certain Simon of Cyrene was compelled to carry
> his cross for him; and this (Simon) was transformed by him (Jesus) so
> that he was thought to be Jesus himself, and was crucified through
> ignorance and error. Jesus, however, took the form of Simon, and
> stood by laughing at them [i.e., those crucifying the Simon now
> transformed to look like Jesus]. For since he was an incorporeal
> power and the Nous [mind] of the unborn Father, he was trans-
> formed in whatever way he pleased. . . ."[12]

> "He assumed that Jesus was born, not of a Virgin, but was the son of
> Joseph and Mary, and came into the world like all other men. . . .
> After baptism, Christ descended on him from the Power above all, in

the form of a dove, whereupon he proclaimed the unknown Father and worked miracles. At the end, the Christ withdrew from Jesus; Jesus suffered, and rose from the dead. Christ, a spiritual being, remained however incapable of suffering.[13]

"The Saviour he assumed to be unbegotten, incorporeal, and without form, but appeared in semblance as a man."[14]

"This is [Christ] who passed through Mary as a water passes through a pipe; and there descended upon him at baptism, in the form of a dove, the savior from the Pleroma (fullness), formed by all the Aeons. . . . he [the heavenly Christ] is said to have remained free of suffering—for it was impossible that he should suffer, since he was unconquerable and invisible—and accordingly, when he [Christ, the son of Mary] was brought before Pilate, the spirit of Christ placed in him [at baptism] was taken away."[15]

"The body (of Christ) which was not real, but merely was seen as an appearance, as these men again affirm. . . ."[16]

"Whilst enduring everything he was continent. Jesus realized divinity: he ate and drank in a special way, without evacuating the food. So great was his power of continence that the food was not corrupted in him, for he did not possess corruptibility."[17]

To the ears of modern readers who have grown up with the later orthodox view that Jesus was at once both divine and human, this seems very strange indeed.[18] But in all fairness to those who lost out in those early theological debates, the seeds of such views can be found in the canonical New Testament. For example, the view of Basilides that Simon of Cyrene suffered instead of Jesus is a possible reading of Mark 15:21–25, even though Mark was trying to describe the crucifixion of Jesus. Moreover, the humanity of Jesus tends to be eclipsed in certain passages in the New Testament having a high Christology, such as John 1:1–18; Phil 2:5–11; Col 1:15–20; these passages portray Jesus as a heavenly figure to such an extent that his human history is all but lost. And the body of Jesus does seem to be something other than human, particularly when Jesus is portrayed as walking on the water (Mark 6:45–50). Such passages with their surreal features drive home with a force the tension between faith and history reflected in the New Testament. These radical explanations of Jesus' person by post-New Testament period writers illustrate the peril of ignoring the personal history of Jesus, the Palestinian Jew. Knowledge of Jesus, as historical man, is not only important for Christian faith, it is absolutely essential to a historical faith. The quest for the historical man keeps the personal history of Jesus from being swallowed up in Christology and mythology, and ensures that the kerygma of the church is anchored in the history of the first century.

∞ RECOMMENDED READING AND SOURCES CONSULTED

FUNK and HOOVER, *The Five Gospels.* HARRIS, *New Testament: A Student's Introduction,* 190–203. HEDRICK, CHARLES W., ed. *The Historical Jesus and the Rejected Gospels. Semeia* 44. Atlanta: Scholars Press, 1988. HEDRICK, *Parables as Poetic Fictions.* MCARTHUR, H. K. *In Search of the Historical Jesus.* New York: Scribners, 1969. NICKLE, *Synoptic Gospels,* 152–66. PERRIN, NORMAN. *Rediscovering the Teaching of Jesus.* New York: Harper & Row, 1967. SCHWEITZER, *Quest of the Historical Jesus.*

∞ ISSUES FOR STUDY AND DISCUSSION

1. *Read the essay by M. Eugene Boring "The Historical-Critical Method's 'Criteria of Authenticity': The Beatitudes in Q and Thomas as a Test Case," Semeia 44 (1988): 9–44. List the criteria and explain the theory behind each one.*

2. *Read the following sayings in Funk and Hoover,* The Five Gospels, *select three and explain why the Jesus Seminar thought they were sayings of Jesus:*

Mark 2:27–28; 4:21; 4:25; 9:50	Luke 11:24–26; 12:6–7; 13:24; 17:20–21
Matt 15:10–11; 19:12; 19:14;	*Gos Thom* 5:2; 6:5; 89; 97; 98
19:23; 22:21	

Be sure to consider all versions of the saying. Do you agree with the rationale? Why? Can the reasons for originality given by Funk and Hoover be equated with any of the criteria in Boring?

3. *Read the following sayings in Funk and Hoover,* The Five Gospels, *select three, and explain why the Jesus Seminar did not think they were sayings of Jesus:*

Mark 2:17b; 12:1–8; 13:28–29	John 12:24–25
Matt 4:19b; 6:22b–23; 7:13–14	*Gos Thom* 3:1–3; 40:1–2; 42:1
13:16–17; 19:21; 24:2	
Luke 6:31; 9:3–4; 11:28; 19:46	

Be sure to consider all versions of the saying. Do you agree with the rationale? Why? Can the reasons for nonoriginality given by Funk and Hoover be equated with any of the criteria in Boring?

4. *Read the following sayings in Funk and Hoover,* The Five Gospels. *The Jesus Seminar rejected these sayings as original with the historical Jesus. What were their reasons? Select two sayings from the list and see if you can offer a plausible argument that they were spoken by the historical Jesus?*

Mark 4:11–12	Luke 9:62
Matt 13:47–50; 26:27–29;	John 3:5–8; 17:1–26
28:18–20	*Gos Thom* 7; 17; 77; 102

5. *Read the following in Funk and Hoover,* The Five Gospels: *Matt 6:9–13 and Luke 11:2–4. How did the Jesus Seminar explain their rather odd color coding of the text of both gospels? Did they think that Jesus prayed the "Lord's Prayer"? What reasons can you give for agreeing or disagreeing with their rationale?*

6. *The most promising place to look for new sayings of the historical Jesus is in the "gray" category of* The Five Gospels. *The members of the Jesus Seminar were divided on whether or not these sayings originated with Jesus. Select three of the following and explain why you think that they are or are not sayings of the historical man:*

Mark 2:21; 4:9, 22–23; 9:1, 40	John 13:20
Matt 7:6; 12:30, 35; 23:24	*Gos Thom* 31:2; 42; 48
Luke 10:21; 12:49	

NOTES

∾ ACKNOWLEDGMENTS (PAGE ix)

1. Thomas J. J. Altizer, "America and the Future of Theology," in Thomas J. J. Altizer and William Hamilton, *Radical Theology and the Death of God* (Indianapolis: Bobbs-Merrill, 1966), 9–21, esp. 9–10.

2. R. W. Funk and Roy Hoover, eds., *The Five Gospels: The Search for the Authentic Words of Jesus* (New York: Macmillan, 1993); R. W. Funk, ed., *The Acts of Jesus* (San Francisco: HarperSanFrancisco, 1998).

∾ PREFACE (PAGES xi–xiii)

1. Dorothy Stimson, *The Gradual Acceptance of the Copernican Theory of the Universe* (Gloucester: Peter Smith, 1972), 58–59.

∾ INTRODUCTION (PAGES xvii–xix)

1. See the characteristics of a scientific view of history in R. G. Collingwood, *The Idea of History* (ed. Jan van der Dusen; rev. ed.; Oxford: Clarendon, 1993), 7–13 (and 14–85).

2. As Scot McKnight appears to do in "Who Is Jesus? An Introduction to Jesus Studies," 62–68, in M. J. Wilkins and J. P. Moreland, eds., *Jesus Under Fire: Modern Scholarship Reinvents the Historical Jesus* (Grand Rapids: Zondervan, 1995).

1. For examples of such miraculous events see E. J. and Ludwig Edelstein, *Asclepius: A Collection and Interpretation of the Testimonies* (2 vols.; Baltimore: Johns Hopkins, 1945), 1:229–37.

2. Philostratus, *The Life of Apollonius of Tyana* (trans. F. C. Conybeare; 2 vols.; London: Heinemann, 1912), 3.38–39; 4.20, 45; 6.42; 7.38. There is even a story of Apollonius's ascension to heaven after his death, as well as post-ascension appearances (2.401–405; 8.30–31).

3. See Conybeare's introduction in Philostratus, *Life of Apollonius*, and the essay by Eusebius, "Against the Life of Apollonius," at the end of the volume.

4. The same charge was leveled against Jesus in Mark 3:22–27.

5. The term *history* has been applied both to the past events themselves and to the historian's reconstruction and sequencing of them. I am using the term in the latter sense.

6. See the entries by R. A. Oden Jr. and Fritz Graf, "Myth," *ABD* 4:946–65; and Leo G. Perdue, "Myth," *MDB*, 593–95.

7. For the *Theogony* see Hugh G. Evelyn-White, *Hesiod: The Homeric Hymns and Homerica* (London: Heinemann, 1977), 78–155. For the *Enuma Elish* see J. B. Pritchard, ed., *The Ancient Near East: An Anthology of Texts and Pictures* (2 vols.; 6th ed.; Princeton: Princeton University Press, 1958), 1:31–39.

8. See the discussion in Henri Frankfort, *Before Philosophy: The Intellectual Adventure of Ancient Man* (Baltimore: Penguin, 1946), 11–36.

9. Homer, *The Iliad* 5.344–346.

10. *Iliad* 16.784–820.

11. *Iliad* 20.438–441.

12. See Frankfort, *Before Philosophy*.

13. According to Aristotle (*Poetics* 15.10), causality in the play (Greek tragedy) should occur in terms of the plot, i.e., in terms of human causation, rather than in terms of a god's actions. The introduction of a god challenged the reality of the presentation and could spoil the effect of the tragedy on the audience (*Poetics* 17.1).

14. From the prism of Sennacherib 2:37–3:49: Pritchard, *Ancient Near East*, 1:199–201; and D. Winton Thomas, ed., *Documents from Old Testament Times* (HarperTorchBooks; New York: Harper & Row, 1958), 64–69.

15. Herodotus, *The Histories* 2.141.

16. See J. Kenneth Kuntz, *The People of Ancient Israel: An Introduction to Old Testament Literature, History and Thought* (New York: Harper & Row, 1974), 307.

17. See Mordechai Cogan and Hayim Tadmor, *II Kings: A New Translation with Introduction and Commentary* (AB 11; New York: Doubleday, 1988), 239.

18. Some early Christians, however, denied the humanity of Jesus, and argued that he only "seemed" to be human. They were therefore called "Docetists" (from the Greek, δοκεῖ, "it seems"). For opposition to this view see the letters of Ignatius and 1 John. For a text that holds this view see the *Gospel of Peter.* For sources that attest to the historicity of Jesus in non-Christian sources see H. C. Kee, *Jesus in History: An Approach to the Study of the Gospels* (2d ed.; New York: Harcourt, Brace, Jovanovich, 1977), 40–54.

19. The Hebrew word translated virgin *('alemāh)* in some modern translations, is also translated as young woman of marriageable age in others. The use of the word elsewhere in the Hebrew Bible seems to support the latter translation (cf. Gen 24:43; Exod 2:8; Prov 30:19; Ps 68:25; Song 1:3; 6:8). The Greek word παρθένος (virgin), however, is used in the Septuagint to translate the Hebrew of Isa 7:14 (but not in the other passages). Matthew's interpretation of Isa 7:14 derives from the Greek text rather than the Hebrew.

20. The Greeks and the Romans likewise had collections of oracular literature; see David E. Aune, *Prophecy in Early Christianity and the Mediterranean World* (Grand Rapids: Eerdmans, 1983), 77–79.

21. See the formula quotations in Matthew (1:22–23; 2:15, 17–18, 23; 4:14–16; 8:17; 12:17–21; 13:14–15, 35; 21:4–5; 27:9–10) and John (10:35; 13:18; 15:25; 17:12; 18:9, 32; 19:24, 28, 36–37; 20:9). See also Acts 2:16–21, 25–28, 30–31. These passages suggest that early Christians believed the events of Jesus' life were predetermined and fixed by God.

22. Thucydides, *History of the Peloponnesian War.* See in particular Book 1.20–23, and compare Homer's *Iliad* and *Odyssey* for examples of human events proceeding with the assistance or interference of the gods.

23. M. A. Fitzsimons, A. G. Pundt, and C. E. Nowell, eds., *The Development of Historiography* (Harrisburg, Pa.: Stackpole, 1954), 13.

24. See James T. Shotwell, "History," *The Encyclopaedia Britannica* (11th ed.; 29 vols.; New York: Encyclopaedia Britannica Co., 1910), 13:527–33.

25. See the discussion in Raymond Brown, *An Introduction to New Testament Christology* (New York: Paulist, 1994), 71–102. There are only two places in the canonical gospels where Jesus unambiguously *accepts* the use of these terms from others: Matt 16:16–17 and Mark 14:61–62. For John 4:25–26 see Brown's discussion, pp. 77–78; see also Mark 8:29–33 and John 20:29.

26. Such as the Apostles' Creed and the Nicene Creed.

27. See Hayden White, *The Content of the Form: Narrative Discourse and Historical Representation* (Baltimore: Johns Hopkins, 1987).

28. See in particular David F. Strauss, *The Life of Jesus Critically Examined* (trans. George Eliot; Philadelphia: Fortress, 1992), 39–92.

29. Northrop Frye, *Anatomy of Criticism: Four Essays* (Princeton: Princeton University Press, 1957), 33.

30. Frye, *Anatomy of Criticism*, 33; see also Charles H. Talbert, *What Is a Gospel? The Genre of the Canonical Gospels* (Philadelphia: Fortress, 1977). Talbert argues that the gospels resemble ancient biographies, since ancient biography also exhibits mythical features similar to the early Christian gospels.

31. Shotwell, "History."

∞ CHAPTER TWO (PAGES 14–29)

1. The undisputed letters are those whose authorship no one seriously questions: Romans, Galatians, 1 Thessalonians, 1 Corinthians, 2 Corinthians, Philippians, and Philemon.

2. In the traditional view (Acts 22:3) Paul studied in Jerusalem "at the feet" of Gamaliel and hence could have known Jesus. But Paul himself refers only to his knowledge of the resurrected Christ (Gal 1:11–17).

3. Analytical study of the gospels as sources is a product of the Enlightenment and certain significant precursors; see William Baird, *From Deism to Tübingen*, vol. 1 of *History of New Testament Research* (2 vols.; Minneapolis: Fortress, 1992), 3–30.

4. The word *critical* means to make judgments in the light of evidence, rather than on the basis of confessional mandates.

5. *Eschatology* means "a study of the last things."

6. *Apocalyptic* is a special kind of eschatology in which there is a cataclysmic end to the cosmic order as it is presently experienced.

7. Compare, for example, Proverbs 8 where Wisdom is personified, the first of the Lord's creation. She enjoyed companionship with God and participated in all his creative acts. Jesus, as one of Wisdom's children (Luke 7:31–35), is one of those in every generation into whom wisdom passes, and thus from this perspective Jesus becomes "a friend of God and prophet" (Wis 7:27–28).

8. The term *Hellenistic antiquity* derives from that culture evolving in the Mediterranean basin following the conquests of the Greek general Alexander the Great (d. 323). It is derived from the Greek name for Greece (Hellas). This culture is to be distinguished from that of classical Greece (Hellenic) and is usually dated 363–31 B.C.E. Hence it is called Hellenistic, i.e., Greek-like. The later culture of the same region (31 B.C.E.–410 C.E.) is called Greco-Roman. The ascendancy of the Roman Empire and its influence on the region added different elements to the cultural mix.

9. For example: Acts 2:22=Mark 1–13; Acts 2:23=Mark 14–15; Acts 2:24=Mark 16.

10. New gospel texts continue to be discovered; see most recently, C. W. Hedrick and Paul A. Mirecki, *The Gospel of the Savior. A New Ancient Gospel* (Santa Rosa, Calif.: Polebridge, 1999).

11. One critical scholar who has argued for earlier dates is J. A. T. Robinson, *Redating the New Testament* (London: SCM, 1976). He dates the present version of John around 65 C.E. and the final stages of the synoptic gospels 50–60 C.E.

12. It is, however, a failed prediction (if it is a prediction) since the temple was destroyed by fire and not by dismantling, as Mark suggests. Even today one can see several stones of Herod's temple one on top of another at the "wailing wall" in Jerusalem. Hence the prediction that "not one stone be left on another" did not occur.

13. Quotations from the New Testament are from the RSV; quotations from *2 Clement* are from *The Apostolic Fathers* (trans. Kirsopp Lake, 2 vols.; LCL; Cambridge: Harvard, 1965).

14. Compare the other titles in the first five books of the Hebrew Bible to those in the Christian Old Testament:

Hebrew Title:	Translation:	Position in first line:	Old Testament title:
Shemoth	"names"	2nd word	Exodus
Wayiqra	"and he called"	1st word	Leviticus
Bemidbar	"in the wilderness"	5th word	Numbers
Debarim	"these are the words"	1st two words	Deuteronomy

15. In John 19:35 and 21:24a the "one who witnessed these things" is said to have given oral testimony about them. In 21:24b the narrator claims that the "disciple bearing witness" has "written these things." This suggests that the present form of the gospel is a text based on the beloved disciple's witness, both oral and written—or at least that is what the narrator thinks.

16. Origen, *Hom. Jer.* 20.3 and *Hom. Luc.* 1 (on Luke 2).

17. The prologue, however, seems to make that claim for Didymos Judas Thomas, the scribe who, it is attested, wrote down "the secret sayings which the living Jesus spoke."

∞ CHAPTER THREE (PAGES 30–47)

1. See Kee, *Jesus in History*, 40–75.

2. The only exception is found in the Caesarean Creed (325), which inserts between Jesus' birth and death the expression: "lived among men." That expression, however, was dropped from the confession that was finally accepted at Nicea. See Henry Bettenson, ed., *Documents of the Christian Church* (2d ed.; Oxford: Oxford University Press, 1963), 23–26.

3. This is the "old Roman creed" of Marcellus, bishop of Ancyra, as quoted in Bettenson, *Documents of the Christian Church*, 23–24.

4. The Romans practiced a cruel form of execution. An individual was nailed to a wooden cross and left to die slowly by gradual suffocation; see V. Tzaferis, "Crucifixion—The Archaeological Evidence," *BAR* 11 (1, 1984): 44–53.

5. A portrait is a re-presenting of a certain subject as it is viewed by a painter, or someone writing a narrative description. It is not the subject as it actually is, but rather the subject as it is seen by the painter. Hence a portrait is an individual's perception.

6. Baptism is immersion of an individual in water. Note the language of Mark 1:10: "and coming up out of the water."

7. As used in the biblical texts "sin" can be defined as "human deviation from the expressed will and desire of God." See E. P. Sanders, "Sin, Sinners," *ABD* 6:31–47.

8. Whether or not Mark attributed to Jesus the power to raise the dead depends on how one reads Mark 5:22–24, 35–43. See C. W. Hedrick, "Miracle Stories as Literary Compositions: The Case of Jairus's Daughter," *Perspectives in Religious Studies* 20 (3, 1993): 217–33.

9. Parables are defined in various ways in contemporary New Testament scholarship. Usually, however, the word *parable* is reserved exclusively for the narratives, or stories, that Jesus told, such as the Good Samaritan (Luke 10:30–35). See the discussion in C. W. Hedrick, *Parables as Poetic Fictions: The Creative Voice of Jesus* (Peabody, Mass.: Hendrickson, 1994), 13–28.

10. The longer ending of Mark (16:9–20) is a later addition to the gospel. In fact four different endings to the Gospel of Mark are attested in the extant manuscripts. See Bruce Metzger, *A Textual Commentary on the Greek New Testament* (New York: United Bible Societies, 1971), 122–28. The shorter ending (16:8) is thought to be the earliest.

11. Eunuchs are males who have been castrated.

12. Joseph was only thought to be Jesus' father (Luke 3:23); Jesus actually had a divine origin (Luke 1:35).

13. John does not use the word *parabolē* (parable) to describe Jesus' teaching style. In John Jesus used *paroimia* (figure, cryptic saying) rather than parables. See Hedrick, *Parables as Poetic Fictions*, 21–22.

14. The term "the living" could be either the resurrected Jesus or the pre-crucifixion Jesus. Both explanations have been suggested. The citations follow the convention of the Meyer translation: J. S. Kloppenborg, M. W. Meyer, S. J. Patterson, and M. G. Steinhauser, *Q-Thomas Reader* (Sonoma, Calif.: Polebridge, 1990).

❧ CHAPTER FOUR (PAGES 48–75)

1. Simply to assume the writings are inspired, infallible, or without error ironically leads the reader to look away from the biblical text itself to resolve aspects in conflict with that belief. Thus, to resolve the differences, some contend that (1) the original documents, the "autographs," had absolutely no inconsistency; or (2) any differences are merely points of view as might be expected from eyewitnesses who report the same event from different perspectives. A third way of reconciling differences is to "harmonize" discrepancies; i.e., to blend the multiple narratives into a single account, or to assert that the event occurred more than once (e.g., Jesus' cleansing of the temple).

2. See chapter 2, note 8 for the term "Greco-Roman." Past understandings of the cultural context of the Gospel of John have regarded it as either Greek or Jewish. But the document reflects aspects of both worlds and in that sense seems to reflect the kind of "Judaism" that one finds in the Dead Sea Scrolls, a collection of "Jewish" writings that reflect the influence of the broader Hellenistic world in its dualism. See J. H. Charlesworth, ed., *John and the Dead Sea Scrolls* (New York: Crossroad, 1990).

3. Gnosticism is a series of eclectic religious movements in the Greco-Roman period. In general it posited a radical breech between the created order of things (the cosmos) and the original source of goodness (God). God did not create the world, but its origin was either a mistake or the deliberate sin of lesser creatures. Humankind is trapped in the cosmos, and only an emissary coming from beyond the world bringing a special knowledge *(gnōsis)* can initiate their release. Hermeticism is religio-philosophical thought that blends Greek philosophical thinking and ancient Egyptian religion. The Dead Sea Scrolls are the writings of a sectarian Jewish community, whose center at Qumran was destroyed in 68–70 C.E. The literature of Gnosticism, Hermeticism, Qumran, and the Gospel of John share a similar outlook on the world, specifically in their dualism. Dualism is the idea that the universe is not a neutral place, but that it is the scene of a moral struggle between the forces of light and darkness, good and evil.

4. The nature miracles are an exception to this trend in Mark: 6:35–52; 8:1–10; 11:12–14, 20–21.

5. This is the interpretation of the incident reported in Mark 3:21–27 that one finds in Matt 12:28=Luke 11:20.

6. Recent New Testament scholarship has argued that the distinction between the author and the narrator, recognized in modern literary theory, should be maintained for the biblical literature as well. The author is the real "flesh and blood" human being who puts the story together in the way that the reader encounters it. The narrator is the narrative voice that the author creates to lead the reader through the story. One should not automatically assume that the narrator and the author are one and the same. See Culpepper, *Anatomy of the Fourth Gospel.*

7. Mark 14:28 and 16:7 anticipate a future meeting of Jesus with his disciples in Galilee. The earliest surviving version of the Gospel of Mark, however, does not include such an appearance. Mark 16:9–20 is not generally regarded as the original ending to Mark's gospel.

8. John's Jesus does use language reminiscent of the traditional words of institution in John 6:52–58. But it is not in connection with the "last meal."

9. This analysis is taken from J. B. Tyson, *A Study of Early Christianity* (New York: Macmillan, 1973), 184–85. In a subsequent revision of the book the classes of material were catalogued by segments, or pericopes:

The New Testament and Early Christianity (1984), 151. In the later publication CLASSES V, VI, and VII are combined into one class: "pericopes in only one gospel."

10. For this discussion see Beare, *Earliest Records*, 29–36.

11. In Matthew Joseph has three additional dreams in which (1) an angel warns him to flee to Egypt to avoid Herod's attempt to kill Jesus (2:13–14); (2) later an angel tells him in a dream that he can return to Israel from Egypt (2:19–21), and (3) finally warned about Archaelaus in a dream (2:22–23), Joseph takes his family to Galilee. Even the wise men have a dream (2:12) warning them about Herod. There is no such cycle of dreams in Luke.

12. See the discussion in Metzger, *Textual Commentary*, 122–26.

13. The third difference lies in the intensive particle καί frequently translated as "even." In this case it is untranslatable and functions merely to intensify the nearness of judgment.

∞ CHAPTER FIVE (PAGES 76–94)

1. For a discussion of how the harmonization worked see Tjitze Baarda, "ΔIAΦΩNIA-ΣΥMΦΩNIA: Factors in the Harmonization of the Gospels, Especially in the Diatessaron of Tatian," in *Gospel Traditions in the Second Century: Origins, Recensions, Text, and Transmission* (ed. W. L. Petersen; Christianity and Judaism in Antiquity 3; Notre Dame: University of Notre Dame Press, 1989), 133–54.

2. See the discussion in Ernest R. Sandeen, *The Roots of Fundamentalism: British and American Millenarianism 1800–1930* (Chicago: University of Chicago Press, 1970), 103–31; and K. C. Boone, *The Bible Tells Them So: The Discourse of Protestant Fundamentalism* (Albany: State University of New York Press, 1989), 23–37.

3. See Henry Hurt, *Reasonable Doubt: An Investigation into the Assassination of John F. Kennedy* (New York: Holt, Rinehart and Winston, 1985), 87–138.

4. There are also other problems. The gospels do not claim to be eyewitnesses, and in fact evidence indicates that they are not. Luke 1:1–4 clearly affirms that the author of that gospel is not an eyewitness. John 21:20–25 and 19:35 speak of an eyewitness in the third person as someone other than the narrator. The earliest tradition about the Gospel of Mark is that Mark was not an eyewitness but that he received his material from Peter, who was thought to be an eyewitness (according to Papias [ca. 130], as reported in Eusebius [early fourth century], *Ecclesiastical History* 3.39.14). The earliest tradition about the Gospel of Matthew is that it was a collection of oracles (i.e., sayings), and our current Gospel of Matthew appears to be a different text in that it is a narrative (Eusebius, *Ecclesiastical History* 3.39.14).

5. See, for example, the foreword by Ray Summers to Fred L. Fisher, *A Composite Gospel* (Nashville: Broadman, 1948), ix.

6. See, for example, A. T. Robertson, *A Harmony of the Gospels for Students of the Life of Christ* (New York: Harper & Brothers, 1922), 25, 156; and Fisher, *Composite Gospel*, 25.

7. See, for example, Josh McDowell, *Evidence That Demands a Verdict* (San Bernardino, Calif.: Campus Crusade for Christ, 1972), 377; and for a more academic argument see Robertson, *Harmony of the Gospels*, 259–62.

8. See the discussion of the synoptic problem in Kümmel, *Introduction to the New Testament*, 38–80.

9. See Kümmel, *Introduction to the New Testament*, 45–47.

10. See the discussion in Kümmel, *Introduction to the New Testament*, 52–56.

11. For other examples, see Matt 23:14 as an assimilation to Mark 12:40 and Luke 20:47; and Luke 17:36 as an assimilation to Matt 24:40. The word *new* in Matt 26:28 and Mark 14:24 has been added by scribes from Luke 22:20. The better known examples are the multiple endings to the Gospel of Mark (16:9–20) and the diverse placements of the pericope of "the woman taken in adultery" that is currently printed in the Gospel of John at 7:53–8:11. It also appears in some manuscripts after John 7:36, 7:44, 21:25, and one manuscript places it after Luke 21:38. See the discussions in Metzger, *Textual Commentary*.

12. See the discussion by Helmut Koester, "History and Development of Mark's Gospel (From Mark to *Secret Mark* and "Canonical" Mark)" in *Colloquy on New Testament Studies: A Time for Reappraisal and Fresh Approaches* (ed. Bruce Corley; Macon, Ga.: Mercer University Press, 1983), 35–57; and for the translation see Miller, ed., *Complete Gospels*, 402–5.

13. Papias, for example, seemed to prefer oral reports over written reports (Eusebius, *Ecclesiastical History* 3.39).

14. For the role of memory in introducing variations into the text see the discussion by Bruce M. Metzger, *The Text of the New Testament: Its Transmission, Corruption, and Restoration* (3d ed.; New York: Oxford University Press, 1992), 87, 192–93, 197–98.

15. Three Greek fragments of parts of the *Gospel of Thomas* exist, but the Coptic version appears to have been a translation of none of the Greek versions represented by these fragments. For the text and translation see Bentley Layton, ed., *Nag Hammadi Codex II, 2–7 Together with XIII, 2*, Brit. Lib. Or 4926 (1), and P. Oxy. 1, 654, 655* (NHS 20–21; 2 vols.; Leiden: E. J. Brill, 1989), 1:95–128.

16. See the argument and the literature in Hedrick, *Parables as Poetic Fictions*, 236–51. There is also an argument for Lukan dependence on sayings influenced by Thomas Christianity. The Thomas tradition is preserved in the *Gospel of Thomas*. Thus "the text of Luke must post-date and be dependent on sayings formed in Thomas Christianity" (G. J. Riley,

"Influence of Thomas Christianity on Luke 12:14 and 5:39," *HTR* 88 [2, 1995]: 229–35).

17. For the view that John did know the synoptic gospels see the discussion in Streeter, *Four Gospels*, 393–426.

18. It is hypothetical in the sense that no early manuscripts exist that contain the text scholars reconstruct as Q. Q scholars, however, object to the designation of the source as "hypothetical," since it has been preserved in Matthew and Luke.

19. The parables that Luke has but Matthew does not are: a Man Going on a Journey (12:36–38), the Prodigal Son/Elder Brother (15:11–32), the Two Sons (21:28a–30), the Two Debtors (7:41–42a), the Samaritan (10:30–35), the Persistent Friend (11:5–8), the Rich Man (12:16b–20), the Barren Fig Tree (13:6b–9), the Tower Builder (14:28–30), the Warring King (14:31–32), the Lost Coin (15:8–9), the Dishonest Steward (16:1b–8), a Rich Man and Lazarus (16:19–31), the Servant (17:7–9), the Unjust Judge (18:2–5), the Pharisee and the Toll Collector (18:10–13).

20. Compare for example,

Matt 9:18–26=Mark 5:21–43=Luke 8:40–56

Matt 8:28–34=Mark 5:1–20=Luke 8:26–39

Matt 17:14–21=Mark 9:14–29=Luke 9:37–43a.

21. See J. C. Hawkins, *Horae Synopticae: Contributions to the Study of the Synoptic Problem* (2d ed. rev.; Oxford: Clarendon, 1968), 117–21.

22. See Hawkins, *Horae Synopticae*, 121–22, and T. J. Weeden, *Mark—Traditions in Conflict* (Philadelphia: Fortress, 1971).

23. Luke's narrative raises the question of who actually baptized Jesus. But the way Luke arranges the imprisonment of John the Baptist immediately before the baptism of Jesus seems to indicate that Luke was trying to put some distance between Jesus and John the Baptist. If Luke intended to convey the idea that John the Baptist actually baptized Jesus, then Luke has done it in a rather careless manner, particularly if Luke was supposed to have seen Matthew's account.

∞ CHAPTER SIX (PAGES 95–109)

1. See for example, James M. Robinson, *Pap. Q* (Claremont, Calif.: Institute for Antiquity and Christianity, 1985). Papyrus was the writing paper of early antiquity. It was made from the stalk of the papyrus plant, which grew along the banks of the Nile River. Strips were cut from the stalk of the plant and soaked in water. One set of strips was laid over another set at right angles to each other, and put under pressure. The result was a highly durable writing surface.

2. See Shawn Carruth and Albrecht Garsky, *Documenta Q: Reconstructions of Q through Two Centuries of Gospel Research Excerpted, Sorted and Evaluated. Q 11:2b–4* (S. D. Anderson, ed.; Leuven: Peeters, 1996) and the report by Milton C. Moreland and James M. Robinson, "The International Q Project: Work Sessions (1995–1996)," *JBL* 116 (3, 1997): 521–25 for examples of the detailed work being done in this regard.

3. For a brief statement see Streeter, *Four Gospels*, 273–75. These five blocks of material have been expanded in later research to thirty-five having a common order; see Kloppenborg, *Formation of Q*, 73.

4. See the discussion in Kloppenborg, *Formation of Q*, 64–80.

5. See the discussion in Kloppenborg, *Formation of Q*, 84–85.

6. Adapted from Kloppenborg, *Q Parallels*. For another recent reconstruction see Jacobson, *First Gospel*.

7. See the brief discussion and bibliography in Jacobson, *First Gospel*, 37–40.

8. See the brief discussion and bibliography in Koester, *Ancient Christian Gospels*, 149–71.

9. Note, for example, the subtitle to the following book: Vaage, *Galilean Upstarts*, 1: "This book seeks to sketch . . . a social profile of Jesus' first followers in Galilee, the earliest form of Christianity known to us, as attested by the initial stratum of Q. . . ."

10. Hence Q is understandable only as a collection coming into existence after Jesus' death. In an oral culture there would have been little interest in a written collection of Jesus' sayings, had he still been living.

11. Scholars are not agreed on the character of the group. Compare the description of Christopher Tuckett in "Q (Gospel Source)," *ABD* 5:567–72, and Vaage, *Galilean Upstarts*, 10–39.

12. See also Robinson, *Jesus of the Sayings Gospel Q*.

✄ CHAPTER SEVEN (PAGES 110–25)

1. See chapter 2, pp. 23–26, "Authorship and Date of the Gospels."

2. Eusebius, *Ecclesiastical History* 3.39.14 in Bettenson, ed., *Documents of the Christian Church*, 27.

3. The Greek word translated "remembered" could be translated: "as he (Peter) related."

4. The standard Papias used to determine that Mark's sequence was not "in order" is unknown.

5. See Eusebius, *Ecclesiastical History* 3.39.

6. But compare 1 Cor 11:23–25 where Paul can attribute to the Lord sayings he undoubtedly received through oral tradition.

7. See the discussion in Calvin J. Roetzel, *The Letters of Paul: Conversations in Context* (3d ed.; Louisville: Westminster John Knox, 1991), 72–82. Paul's language also echoes sayings of Jesus known from the

canonical gospels (Roetzel, *Letters of Paul*, 77–79) and the *Gospel of Thomas* (saying 17=1 Cor 2:9). Also compare Gal 1:11–12, and especially 2 Cor 12:9, where Paul claims that certain information about Jesus came directly from the Lord.

8. See, for example, the journal *Oral Tradition*, published since 1986.

9. Kelber, *Oral and Written Gospel*, 1–2.

10. See the review article by Albert B. Lord, "Perspectives on Recent Work on Oral Literature," in *Oral Literature: Seven Essays* (ed. J. J. Duggan; New York: Harper & Row, 1975), 1–24.

11. See the brief but lucid discussion by Thomas, *Literacy and Orality in Ancient Greece*, 29–51.

12. See Hermann Gunkel, *The Legends of Genesis: The Biblical Saga and History* (New York: Shocken Books, 1964 [1st German ed., 1901]).

13. Karl Ludwig Schmidt, *Der Rahmen der Geschichte Jesu: Literarkritische Untersuchungen zur Ältesten Jesusüberlieferung* (Berlin: Trowitzsch & Sohn, 1919). Unfortunately Schmidt's work has never been translated into English.

14. See Kelber, *Oral and Written Gospel*, 1–8.

15. See Kelber, *Oral and Written Gospel*, 3. Bultmann throughout noted certain tendencies of the synoptic tradition: dogmatic motifs, novelistic embellishments, the law of single perspective, the rule of scenic duality, an inclination toward differentiation and individualization, transposition of material into direct speech, and the law of repetition.

16. The gospels themselves document a period following the crucifixion when the disciples had not yet come to believe in the resurrection: Luke 24; John 20–21; John 2:22.

17. See the excellent brief discussion of this process by Nickle, *Synoptic Gospels*, 11–32. Others have objected that this view of oral transmission is entirely too negative, and have proposed a more optimistic model that ensures the traceability of the synoptic tradition back in "an unbroken path" to Jesus himself; see Gerhardsson, *Origins of the Gospel Traditions*. See the review of both of these positions by Kelber, *Oral and Written Gospel*, 3–14.

18. Adapted from Kelber, *Oral and Written Gospel*, 14–34 and used by permission.

19. For this reason, Kelber notes, Bultmann's contention that the Jesus tradition began only with the resurrection faith of the earliest disciples is doubtful. In other words, some part of the Jesus tradition likely antedated the resurrection.

20. This section is adapted from Tyson, *New Testament and Early Christianity*, 212–19.

21. For the full form of the early Christian kerygma see Dodd, *Apostolic Preaching and Its Development*.

22. See the parallels collected by A. Plummer, *A Critical and Exegetical Commentary on the Gospel According to St. Luke* (New York: Scribners, 1920), 126.

23. Aramaic is a Semitic dialect similar to Hebrew, and Hebrew is the language in which the Jewish holy Scriptures are written. After the death of Alexander the Great, his kingdom was divided among his generals. Initially Seleucus gained control of Syria and Mesopotamia, but later the Seleucid kingdom came to control Palestine as well. Aramaic was the language of government and commerce in the Seleucid kingdom, and it became the language of first-century Palestine as part of what it inherited from the Seleucids.

24. On this issue see the article by Thomas E. Boomershine, "Jesus of Nazareth and the Watershed of Ancient Orality and Literacy," in Dewey, *Orality and Textuality*, 7–36.

25. See the discussion in Metzger, *Text of the New Testament*, 186–206.

26. For a brief discussion of these narrative units see Tyson, *New Testament and Early Christianity*, 219–31.

27. For other collections of sayings, see Matt 18 and 23; Mark 13; and *Did.* 1:2–6.

28. There are other "collections" of parables: in *Gos Thom*, logia 63, 64, 65; 96, 97, 98; 107, 109. See the *Apocryphon of James*, Nag Hammadi Codex I,2:8,4–27, which seems to presuppose a parables collection.

29. Looking for theological tendencies among the evangelists is called "redaction criticism." The term means "[a study of] the history of editing [of the gospels]."

30. See the discussion in Metzger, *Text of the New Testament*, 190–95.

∞ CHAPTER EIGHT (PAGES 126–34)

1. See Aune, *Prophecy in Early Christianity*, 103–52.

2. See in particular Aune, *Prophecy in Early Christianity*.

3. See Aune, *Prophecy in Early Christianity*, 23–48, 82–85.

4. See Boring, *Continuing Voice of Jesus*, 50–51, for other contrasts between early Christian and Hellenistic prophets.

5. 1 Cor 7:10–40 is frequently cited as evidence that the early Christians did make such a distinction; see the discussion in Boring, *Continuing Voice of Jesus*, 28–29.

6. As Boring recognizes; see *Continuing Voice of Jesus*, 38: This does not "exclude the prophet's utilization of sources, traditional material, or the reflection of the prophet himself or herself, all of which may be involved in the personal formulation and delivery to the community of what he or she perceives to be directly revealed from the risen Lord."

7. See the survey of the literature in Boring, *Continuing Voice of Jesus*, 59–85, and idem, *Sayings of the Risen Jesus*, 22–52. See also, Aune, *Prophecy in Early Christianity*, 189–231, 247–90.

8. Acts reflects Luke's view of Christian origins. It is the only early Christian reflection on Christian origins that we have in the literature. Acts is generally dated around 80–90 C.E. and hence must be considered

as secondary information for the period 30 to 70. It is, however, a primary source for determining how the church in the latter part of the first century viewed the character and history of the church in the first half of the century. And some scholars are more optimistic about its general picture of the prophets. For example, see Boring, *Continuing Voice of Jesus*, 65, 77.

9. Boring, *Continuing Voice of Jesus*, 61.

10. See Aune, *Prophecy in Early Christianity*, 249–50.

11. See Aune, *Prophecy in Early Christianity*, 251; see also 252–60 for additional sayings Aune describes as possible oracles in Paul's writings.

12. Matt 28:9–10 appears to be a word of the resurrected Lord that parallels an earlier word of the historical man: to Matt 28:10 compare Matt 26:32.

13. In this connection the visions that follow in Rev 4:1–22:5 are also appropriate to the prophetic experience. In some ways they are similar to what Paul alludes to in 2 Cor 12:2–4.

14. For example, to Rev 2:27 compare Ps 2:9, and to Rev 3:3 compare 1 Thess 5:2.

15. Here we are only considering the synoptic gospels. Identifying the traditional sayings in the Gospel of John is far more difficult, and little work has been done in this regard. See the discussion in Boring, *Continuing Voice*, 266–68.

16. Boring, *Continuing Voice of Jesus*, 230 (191–234). An equally large number of Q sayings also appear to Boring to have been sayings of Jesus the historical man reformulated by early Christian prophets: Q 6:20b–21; 10:2, 23–24; 11:14–23, 29a, 31–32; 12:2–7, 22–34, 51–56, 57–59; 13:23–30; 17:23–35 (p. 231).

17. See Boring, *Sayings of the Risen Jesus*, 183–95, and idem, *Continuing Voice of Jesus*, 235–42.

18. Boring, *Sayings of the Risen Jesus*, 204–16, and idem, *Continuing Voice of Jesus*, 247–55.

19. Boring *Sayings of the Risen Jesus*, 219–26, and idem, *Continuing Voice of Jesus*, 257–62.

20. Compare Aune, *Prophecy in Early Christianity*, 247–48, for three different criteria.

21. For his characteristics of early Christian prophetic speech see *Continuing Voice of Jesus*, 155–86, and idem, *Sayings of the Risen Jesus*, 111–36.

22. *Sayings of the Risen Jesus*, 186. I have translated Boring's Greek and revised his statement slightly. Compare *Continuing Voice of Jesus*, 236.

23. Boring also argues that early Christian prophets have influenced the Jesus tradition in several ways; see M. E. Boring, "Christian Prophecy and the Sayings of Jesus: The State of the Question," *NTS* 29 (1983): 109–10.

24. See Gillespie, *First Theologians*, 6–20. Boring seems to be rather optimistic that we can identify such sayings and surveys the synoptic tra-

dition for them. Aune, on the other hand, is more skeptical (*Prophecy in Early Christianity*, 247, and 233–45) and does not survey the synoptic gospels for such sayings.

∞ CHAPTER NINE (PAGES 135–51)

1. See Schweitzer, *Quest of the Historical Jesus*, 13–26, and Talbert, ed., *Reimarus: Fragments*.

2. M. Eugene Boring describes the criteria that have been used to bridge the gap: "The Historical-Critical Method's 'Criteria of Authenticity': The Beatitudes in Q and Thomas as a Test Case," *Semeia* 44 (1988): 9–44. Boring summarizes the various criteria and adds two of his own. In the last chapter of the *Semeia* volume, John Dominic Crossan proposes a new criterion: "Divine Immediacy and Human Immediacy: Toward a New First Principle in Historical Jesus Research," 121–40. Clearly, new criteria will emerge in the future.

3. A recent publication by the Jesus Seminar addresses the issue of Jesus' deeds: R. W. Funk and the Jesus Seminar, *The Acts of Jesus: What Did Jesus Really Do?* (San Francisco: HarperSanFrancisco, 1998).

4. For an example of the process of validating individual sayings from the Johannine discourses see Helmut Koester, "Gnostic Sayings and Controversy Traditions in John 8:12–59," pp. 97–110 in *Nag Hammadi, Gnosticism, and Early Christianity* (ed. C. W. Hedrick and R. Hodgson Jr.; Peabody, Mass.: Hendrickson, 1986).

5. Boring, for example, regards Matt 5:18 as a saying of an early Christian prophet (*Sayings of the Risen Jesus*, 174). The Markan passion predictions he regards as probably originating with post–Easter Christianity (*Sayings of the Risen Jesus*, 183).

6. Perrin (*Rediscovering the Teaching of Jesus*, 46) following H. K. McArthur, ("Basic Issues: A Survey of Recent Gospel Research," p. 140 in *In Search of the Historical Jesus*, ed. H. K. McArthur) pointed to the motif of "Jesus' love for tax collectors and sinners" as meeting this criterion, but this is questionable as "tax collectors and sinners" are only to be found in the synoptic tradition. They are not found in Q, *Gospel of Thomas*, or John.

7. R. W. Funk, Bernard Brandon Scott, James R. Butts, *The Parables of Jesus, Red Letter Edition. A Report of the Jesus Seminar* (Sonoma, Calif.; Polebridge, 1988).

8. See Funk and Hoover, *The Five Gospels*, 524–25.

9. The idea that the iota and hook represent translations of original Hebrew (or Aramaic) letters does not work quite as well. To remain true to the image in Greek the Greek iota needs replacing with the Hebrew yodh, since iota is the smallest Greek letter and yodh the smallest Hebrew letter. In that case, the most likely candidate for the hook then becomes the waw, which is not a good parallel. Perhaps the hook could be understood as the serif used to distinguish similar Hebrew letters from one another. But

there is no way to know if the saying was composed first in Aramaic and then translated into Greek. It could as easily have been composed in Greek.

10. See Nickle, *Synoptic Gospels*, 164–66.

11. For example, Crossan's criterion of "adequacy" and Boring's criteria of "plausible *Traditionsgeschichte*" and "hermeneutical potential"; see *Semeia* 44 (1988): 23–24, 125.

12. Attributed to Basilides by Irenaeus: W. Foerster, *Gnosis: A Selection of Gnostic texts* (R. McL. Wilson, trans.; 2 vols.; Oxford: Clarendon Press, 1972), 1.60

13. Cerinthus according to Irenaeus: R. Haardt, *Gnosis: Character and Testimony* (J. F. Hendry, trans.; Leiden: E. J. Brill, 1971), 63.

14. Saturninus according to Irenaeus: Foerster, *Gnosis*, 1:41.

15. Ptolemaus according to Irenaeus: Foerster, *Gnosis*, 1:139–40; cf. 152.

16. The Archontics according to Epiphanius: Foerster, *Gnosis*, 1:298.

17. Valentinus according to Clement of Alexandria: Foerster, *Gnosis*, 1.242.

18. The later orthodox creeds specifically rejected such a dehistoricized position; see Bettenson, *Documents of the Christian Church*, 24–26.

INDEX OF MODERN AUTHORS

ANCIENT LITERATURE

Early Christian Authors